LIGHT ON DUMYAT

Light On
DUM-Y-AT

Rennie McOwan

THE SAINT ANDREW PRESS
EDINBURGH

First published in 1982 by
THE SAINT ANDREW PRESS
121 George Street, Edinburgh EH2 4YN

Copyright ©Rennie McOwan 1982

ISBN 0 7152 0544 7

Printed in Hong Kong by
Permanent Typesetting & Printing Co., Ltd.

CONTENTS

FOR
Lesley, Michael, Tom and Niall

1 Northwards Bound

The owl sat alertly on the pine-tree branch, and stirred uneasily.

The dawn wind whispered softly through the branches and ruffled the owl's feathers. Scudding clouds held back the morning sun, and the woods were gloomy and black.

A man lay at the bottom of the tree. He did not see the owl, hidden in the branches. Even the yellow glow of its searching eyes did not penetrate the darkness.

The man was busy. He lay full length, dressed in black clothing. His face and hands were covered in black soot so that he blended with his surroundings. The owl prepared for flight as the man pushed and pulled at the dead brushwood and branches lying around, and arranged them in a screen in front of him.

The man pulled binoculars out of a rucksack, and began to polish the lenses with a handkerchief he took from his pocket. The owl launched itself from the tree and glided silently through the branches, seeking a safer place to hole up during the day.

The sun grew brighter, as the man parted the branches and examined the view ahead. The fringe of woodland lay at the top of a hill. From it he could look over rolling countryside, part heathery moor, part green and fertile farmland and part forest. Small white-washed farms nestled in protected hollows.

The grey stones of a large mansion house dominated the foreground and in the distance were the buildings of a large town. It was a peaceful scene.

Then, in the distance, came the agonised wail of a train whistle. The man craned forward as the roar of the diesel engine was heard faintly.

His binoculars closely scrutinised the mansion house.

He saw the door open and a woman come out. She got into an estate car which lay parked beside the front door. In the stillness of the summer morning he heard the car door slam and the engine start. The car disappeared round a bend in the drive.

The man took out a notebook and wrote busily in it. Then he settled down in his den of branches and continued his vigil. Now and again he moved uncomfortably, and his face was angry.

Gavin could not make up his mind whether to be an Ancient Pict or an Ancient Roman. Both had lived and fought in the hills where he was going.

As the train chugged northwards towards Scotland he passed the time by sleeping or by examining the luggage he was taking on holiday. He had not wanted to go to Scotland, but had little choice.

He remembered the day well when a letter came cancelling the family holiday. His mother had come into the dining room with an envelope in her hand. She stood beside the breakfast table for a moment. Then she told him the bad news.

"Gavin, I am very, very sorry but we cannot go on holiday to Anglesey as planned," she said. "Daddy has been called away on business and I must stay at home for part of the time."

"Can't I stay at home too?" Gavin asked.

"Well, dear, there would be nothing for you to do. But you could go to Uncle Fergus's house in Scotland. You would like that. He lives in a large house beside the hills. You could camp and climb and have plenty of fun."

Gavin considered this for a moment. At Anglesey they were going to stay in a cottage and swim and play in an old boat Daddy had bought. Scotland seemed rather tame, but he decided he might as well go.

"Why don't you write to Aunt Elspeth and ask her about the house and the hills," suggested mother.

So Gavin sent a letter. It was short. He hoped Aunt Elspeth was well, said he was looking forward to coming, and what luggage should he bring?

Aunt Elspeth's letter surprised him. It was typed. Gavin had never had a typed letter before. It was also long. It covered four pages of notepaper.

Gavin took the letter up to his bedroom, sprawled on his bed, and read what Aunt Elspeth had to say.

She wrote: "You will like it here. There is no one in the house but Uncle Fergus and myself. He is writing a book so you won't see much of him. In fact, I am using his typewriter.

"You can stay in the spare room in the tower. It is right at the top and looks over the woods.

"Nearby are the Ochil hills. They are quite lonely. No one lives there except some sheep and a fox or two.

"If you are interested in bird-watching, it is a splendid place. There are curlews on the moors, owls in the woods and hawks and buzzards on the hills.

"Be sure and bring strong boots, an anorak-jacket and plenty of old clothes.

"There are many places to explore, including some old silver mines in the hills. They are quite safe. All the dangerous tunnels have been blocked up."

Gavin threw down the letter. His eyes gleamed. He was thrilled. Lonely hills. Woods to explore. Silver mines. And birds!

Recently he had got quite interested in birds and had visited the London museums identifying the species he saw in his garden and in the parks.

He picked up the letter again.

"I am afraid there are not many children nearby, but I expect you will meet some friends.

"If you want to, I will take you into Stirling — which is a former capital of Scotland — and you can visit the Castle and see the guns."

Gavin wriggled with pleasure. A castle nearby. And guns. Scotland sounded better and better.

His mind was made up. He would spend the holiday being an explorer. It was almost as if Aunt Elspeth could read his mind. He read on.

"Long ago," she wrote, "ancient tribes lived in the hills. They were known as Picts and were very fierce warriors. They wore clothes made of skins and painted themselves, rather like the Indians you see on television.

"The Romans when they conquered Britain also came to these hills, but they were never able to settle for long. The Picts defeated them in battle."

Aunt Elspeth went on: "I don't know whether you are interested in all this or not, but I know boys like to explore and play games, so perhaps you can play at being a Pict or a Roman."

Gavin put down the letter. Aunt Elspeth sounded a sport. Yes, he would go to Scotland. He shouted downstairs: "Yes, Mother, I'd love to go."

And so it was arranged.

Gavin sat with his face pressed to the window as the train ran through green fields and small towns.

Gradually the landscape changed, taking on a harsher look. Grass gave way to stretches of moorland covered in heather and gorse. Little lochs winked in the sunlight. On the horizon rose a rampart of blue hills.

Gavin hauled his case and rucksack from the rack and spread his clothes over the seat. It was the sixth time since leaving London he had done this. He could not get over the thrill of his new equipment.

Mother, still feeling he was sorry about not going to Anglesey, had taken him to a large mountaineering shop where eyes were dazzled by rows of anoraks in bright red, orange, blue and green, and shelves of tough-looking mountaineering boots. Trays held metal rock-climbing equipment, whistles and a variety of knives and cooking equipment. Gavin wandered around in a happy daze while mother made purchases.

Now, against the background of the chugging train,

4

he spread his new equipment out on the seat and gloated.

One dark green anorak. Gavin had rejected the bright colours. The assistant had said they were bright so that they could be seen on the hills. "If climbers have an accident, they can easily be seen," he said.

Gavin almost said he was an ancient Pict and did not want to be seen. But what he said was: "I am very keen on bird-watching and want to be camouflaged."

"Oh, in that case, a green one would be best," said the assistant and wrapped up the green anorak. "If you're a bird-watcher, sir, you might like to look through our book section," he added.

So Gavin, blushing at being called 'sir', went through to a nearby room and examined the piles of books stacked from floor to ceiling. He had saved his pocket money for many weeks since Aunt Elspeth's letter came, so he carefully counted it out. He found he had enough for three small books. He bought a pocket-sized book of birds, a book on animal tracks and a book on hill-walking and camping. His mother paid for the other equipment.

Putting his anorak down on the carriage seat, Gavin opened up the pockets. In one was a compass with a luminous dial and arrow. He had already tried it out under the bedclothes in his room.

In another was a mountaineer's torch with a head-set rather like a miner's lamp. Three loops went over his head with the torch sitting just above his forehead. The flex went over his shoulder into a battery case which was inside the rucksack. The battery case could also be used as a separate hand-torch.

The beauty of the head-torch was that it could be worn while the hands were free to climb or to do anything else. Very necessary for an explorer, Gavin thought. Especially one who might explore a silver mine.

He pulled out his new boots. They were brown with

rubber soles deeply cut into an indented pattern to prevent slipping. Although they were heavy, they hardly made any sound.

In another pocket of his anorak were a whistle and a black knife. The knife had two blades, a tin opener and a file.

Gavin kept his best treasures to the last. Mother had bought him a sleeping bag and a set of dixies, in case he got the chance to cook on a wood fire out of doors.

The set of dixies did not look very much at first sight. Actually, Gavin thought, it looked just like one pan. But when one opened it up, there was another, smaller pan fitted inside and a cup inside that.

Inside the aluminium cup was a small egg-shaped holder with little holes in it. It was for boiling tea. One put the leaves inside the holder and dropped it into a pan of boiling water. It had a little chain and hook for pulling it out. Also inside the pan was a strong clamp, for gripping hot pans. It was called a bulldog.

Gavin laid them out in a row. It seemed impossible that so much could be within one aluminium pan. He counted them. One frying pan (which was the outside piece) with its handle which closed the lid of the whole set. One deep cooking pan with lid (which could also be used as a plate). One cup. One tea strainer. One bulldog.

He put them together again, closed the handle with a satisfying clang and stowed them in his rucksack.

The sleeping bag was very expensive. It was made of quilted down and tapered towards the foot. Once one got into it, little tapes at the top pulled it tight around the shoulders. It was very warm. Gavin had spent one night in it to try it out.

He was so busy examining his equipment that, when he next looked out of the window, the train was near the edge of a town and he could see what looked like a large river nearby.

Gavin tugged open the door and leapt into the

corridor. Above the roofs of the houses was a large crag. On it stood a castle. On a little hill nearby, he could see two cannon. In the distance he could see hills.

Next minute, the train was slowing to a halt in a large station.

"Stirling! Stirling!" shouted a porter as he passed the window.

Gavin grabbed his case, swung his rucksack on his back and set off for the ticket entrance. He had that excited feeling that began every holiday.

What he did not know was that he was about to start the most exciting time of his entire life.

2 The Mysterious Light

Before Gavin could gather his wits, hands grabbed his case.

"I'm Aunt Elspeth," said a voice.

Standing in front of him was a pleasant-looking lady of about mother's age. She was wearing a tweed skirt and jacket and had a little green hat on her head.

"You must be Gavin," she said. "You are very welcome. Give me your case and rucksack and we'll put them in the car."

She led the way out of the station into a yard. In one corner was a large van. Aunt Elspeth opened the back doors and heaved Gavin's luggage inside.

"Hop in the front," she said. Gavin carefully opened the door on his side and made himself comfortable.

Soon they were driving through the streets of the town, skipping past lorries and vans. Once a flock of sheep blocked the road, and they had to wait until the shepherd and two boys herded them past. In another street, Gavin saw lorries with horses and cattle in the back.

"It's market day," said Aunt Elspeth. "All the farmers come into Stirling to sell their sheep and pigs. Their wives come too and shop. It's very busy today. However, it is quiet where we live."

Soon they left the houses behind. The road narrowed and began twisting uphill. He liked the way Aunt Elspeth drove, swinging the van deftly round the bends.

As they drove along Gavin gazed eagerly from side to side. On each side of the road were large woods of firs and spruce, dark green and black. Behind them he could see the tops of hills, grey and scattered with boulders.

Suddenly, Aunt Elspeth turned the car sharply off the

road and through a gate bounded on either side by two huge stone pillars.

"This is our drive," she said. "It runs through the woods for about half a mile to the house. There's nobody here but us. There's a farm over the hill which can be reached by a path through the woods."

"Nobody at all?" said Gavin. Surely *somebody* must live nearby.

Aunt Elspeth glanced at him.

"Oh, you won't be lonely," she said. "There are some children on the farm and a bus passes the end of the drive twice a day. You can go into Stirling at any time you want." She gave him a kindly glance. "Whenever you feel like a jaunt, let me know. We keep a maid at the house and she helps with the meals, so I'll be able to come with you sometimes. Have you any special plans?"

"Yes," said Gavin. "I want to explore the hills."

"The hills? Well, you'll have a splendid time. But don't go out of sight of the house, will you, until you know the area? People have been lost there. We don't want to spoil your holiday by calling out a search party for you."

Gavin reached over the seat and put his hand in his rucksack pocket. He produced the compass.

Aunt Elspeth laughed: "I see you are prepared. Can you use it?"

Gavin nodded. He had practised using a compass and map in a park at home.

"Well, it's an early bed tonight," said Aunt Elspeth. "Tomorrow I'll make you some sandwiches and a flask of tea and you can explore as much as you like."

The car stopped in front of a large stone house. Gavin eyed it with interest. It had two storeys and a high roof. At one end was a square tower, with real battlements. Ivy covered most of the tower. It had one window near the top. Aunt Elspeth saw him looking.

"That's your window," she said. "And if you feel

9

like climbing down the ivy — don't! It's not very strong. I don't want to write to your mother telling her you have had an accident."

For the second time that day, Gavin promised to be careful.

A pebble-covered drive ran right round the house, with large flower beds in front. The woods pressed round on all sides. They looked deep and peaceful. Gavin listened in delight. There was no sound, but a soft whispering from the trees and the deep crooning of wood pigeons in the distance.

The rest of the day passed in a sleepy haze. Gavin was tired by his journey.

Aunt Elspeth led the way to his room. It was small, with thick walls papered in bright colours. His bed was against one wall.

"These are the Ochil hills," said Aunt Elspeth, pointing out of the window.

Gavin peered out. Beyond the trees and dwarfing the house lay a range of hills. They were like a huge, frozen green wave, he thought.

He studied their steep flanks, seamed with little cliffs and covered with clumps of gorse and boulders. Half hidden by a clump of tall pine trees, he could make out a rocky pointed peak at the end of the range.

"What's that?" he asked Aunt Elspeth.

She came over to the window.

"Oh, that's Dumyat," she said. "Long ago there was a tribe of Picts called the Maeatae. They built a fort on top of that hill. It overlooks the Forth valley and then northwards to the Grampian mountains.

"A Pictish fort is called a dun," she continued. So that's how the hill got its name. The dun of the Maeatae. Since then, the name has become slurred into Dumyat. Pronounced Dum-eye-at."

"Aunt Elspeth," said Gavin. "How do you know all this?"

"Oh, I used to roam these hills too when I was a girl," she said. "I love the hills. So do you, I think. It must be your mother's blood in you. She loved the hills as well."

Aunt Elspeth laughed. "Some of your cousins didn't. When they came to stay here, they couldn't sleep. They thought the hills were going to fall on them!"

Gavin chuckled. Yet he could understand their feelings. The hills did appear to lean over the house. They "frowned", he thought.

"You can meet Uncle Fergus in the morning," said Aunt Elspeth. Now, get to sleep. I'll call you early and show you over the house. You'll have plenty of time to explore."

Gavin lay in his narrow bed and gazed at the hills. Now that it was dark they were just a blue-black mass against the sky. A few stars twinkled palely. Dark night clouds drifted slowly across the sky.

It was then that his adventure began. Halfway up the hill — the peak Aunt Elspeth had called Dumyat — he suddenly saw a light. It winked for a moment and then disappeared.

Gavin lay still. It must have been a shooting star. Or his imagination. Then the light appeared again. It flashed twice and then disappeared.

Gavin jumped out of bed. He opened the window quietly and leaned out. All was still. From a farm, a dog barked twice. The pines sighed softly. From the woods came the hoot of a tawny owl.

Gavin studied the hills again. They remained black and silent. Then the light flashed again. He saw it clearly.

But who would have a light up there? No one lived there. Aunt Elspeth had said so. Could it be poachers? Or smugglers? Anyhow, no one burned a light late at night in those lonely hills without good reason.

Then an idea struck him. Tomorrow he would climb Dumyat and see if he could find out what the mysterious

11

light was. It would give him something to do. He could try out his new equipment.

He wouldn't say anything to Aunt Elspeth. He would enjoy the mystery himself. Once he found out, he could tell her.

As sleep overcame him, one thought was uppermost in his mind. How to find the light. He struggled out of bed again. Reaching for his anorak, he searched through the pocket. Out came a pencil.

Peering up at Dumyat, he scribbled a tiny arrow on the wallpaper at the side of the window. It pointed to where he had last seen the light.

It was a funny sort of light, thought Gavin as he drifted off to sleep. It was almost as if someone had opened the door of a lighted room and then shut it again. Quickly.

3   The Search Begins

Gavin raced downstairs the next morning and burst into the kitchen.

"Good morning!" he shouted.

Aunt Elspeth swung round from the stove. Betty, the maid, looked up from setting the table and smiled at the eager figure.

"I see you are ready to explore," said his aunt.

She examined him. He wore his green anorak, a khaki open-neck shirt, long trousers tucked into long socks and his new boots. His socks were folded down over the top of his boots. Gavin had seen this in a picture in the mountaineering shop. He thought it very dashing. On his back was his rucksack.

Earlier he had laid his equipment out on his bed and checked it. He made out a list in a hard-covered notebook he had bought to write down the names of any new birds he saw. He printed: one torch and spare battery, one cagoule (in case there was heavy rain), one compass, one map, one knife, one whistle, one bird book. He scored each one off as he put it in the rucksack.

As he tucked into his breakfast, Aunt Elspeth questioned him on his journey.

"I'm going to the top of Dumyat," said Gavin, his mouth full of toast.

"Oh, you are, are you," said Aunt Elspeth. "What route are you taking?"

What route? Gavin paused. He had not planned a route. He was simply going to walk through the woods and then try and find the easiest way to the top.

Aunt Elspeth saw him hesitate.

"Once you've finished your breakfast and seen over the house, I'll show you how to plan a route on your

map. Don't worry, we'll go over the house quickly and then you can be off. Besides, you've got to meet your Uncle Fergus.''

She handed him a flask of tea, a packet of sandwiches and some fruit. Gavin put them in his rucksack and adjusted the straps. It sat very well on his back: nice and tightly.

"It's best to keep your rucksack fairly tight," said Aunt Elspeth. "Then it won't swing about and bump you. Come on, let's go and say hello to Uncle Fergus. He's working in the library."

Gavin was so excited about thinking about the mysterious light that he paid little attention to the house. He vaguely remembered passing through large rooms and along dim corridors. Then Aunt Elspeth opened the door to the library.

Gavin gasped. The walls were covered in shelves of books. A row of antlered deer heads were fastened to one wall. But it was not that which took his breath away.

A large table stood in the middle of the floor, covered in silver ornaments. There were plates and cups, stemmed objects like vases, all piled up in a glittering heap.

An elderly man got up from the desk and came towards them.

"You must be Gavin," he said, shaking Gavin's hand.

"How do you do, sir," said Gavin politely.

Uncle Fergus smiled kindly at him.

"There's no need to call me sir. Just call me Uncle. I'm afraid I won't see much of you this week. Aunt Elspeth has probably told you that I am writing a book about the ancient silver treasures of Scotland. I hope to have most of my notes done soon. After that we'll have some fun. Eh?''

He poked Gavin playfully in the chest.

"Yes, Uncle," said Gavin. "Thank you very much."

15

He went on: "Can I ask you a question?"

"Certainly," said Uncle Fergus. "Ask me anything you like. But I can guess. It'll be about the silver. It always has that effect on people."

"Did the silver for these ornaments come from the Ochil hills," asked Gavin. "Aunt Elspeth said there were old mines in the hills."

Uncle Fergus nodded.

"Centuries ago some ornaments were made from silver from here. But the silver was quickly worked out. The old miners also looked for gold, but didn't find any. Not very many ornaments were made. I have two here, both on loan from museums."

He lifted up two shallow bowls with little handles at each end.

"What are they?" Gavin asked.

"They are ancient quaichs," said Uncle Fergus.

Then, seeing Gavin was still looking puzzled, he went on: "They were used for ceremonial drinking, for toasts and so on."

He picked up another. It had a fragile, battered appearance.

"This may be a chalice and might have come from a church. That is one of the things I am trying to find out."

Gavin looked again at the glittering array. There were cups, bowls, plates and cutlery. He thought he saw a pistol. Uncle Fergus picked it up, and put it down again inside a wooden box.

"Very valuable," he said with a smile. "A unique specimen of a Scottish Doune pistol, faced with silver."

"Is it all valuable?" asked Gavin. "Supposing someone stole it."

"It's valuable all right," said Uncle Fergus. "But no one is going to steal it here. No one knows I have the museum pieces in the house — other than museum officials, that is — and the rest of the silver is our own. It belonged to the family. It has been here for centuries.

16

It's locked up each night in our safe."

He pointed to a large safe in one corner.

"Besides," he went on, "the library windows are barred. The keys to the outside door are kept in my study each night." He returned to his desk.

Gavin could see that Uncle Fergus wanted to get on with his work. So he shook his hand again, said goodbye, and walked towards the door.

Just above the door was a large oil painting. The light from the library window glinted on it, so Gavin stepped sideways to get a better look.

It was a very dramatic picture. It showed a group of Highlanders in bright red tartan standing in a ring round a torn flag. They were being attacked by hundreds of soldiers. Most of the Highlanders were wounded.

"What's that?" he asked Aunt Elspeth. She glanced up.

"Oh, that's a painting of the Clan MacRae at the Battle of Sheriffmuir. The battlefield is not far from here. We can visit it if you like.

The MacRae Clan came from far in the north-west, from an area known as Kintail," she continued. "They had a boast that they never left a battlefield while their flag still flew. At Sheriffmuir, they stayed when their comrades fled and were killed to a man."

Gavin blinked. What a fierce lot they were hundreds of years ago! Picts fighting Romans and driving them back. Highlanders dying for the sake of a flag. It was difficult to believe it had all happened in these quiet hills.

"That's enough of touring the house," said Aunt Elspeth. "Come on downstairs and I'll show you how your map works."

She and Gavin went out of the front door and knelt down on the lawn. Gavin spread his new map out.

"Get your compass out," said his aunt.

Gavin laid it on the grass and watched until the needle

quivered backwards and forwards and then stopped. He turned the compass slowly until the needle was in line with the little marking which indicated the north.

"Well, what you do now is to make sure the top of your map sheet is also at the north." She pushed the map round until the top edge was beside the north sign on the compass.

"Remember," she said. "The top of your map is always north. Now the next thing to do is to work out a route."

Gavin and his aunt bent over the map.

"If you go through the woods, a path will bring you out at an old zigzag road which will lead you to the top of a small hill called Craigomas. It is called that because people used to dig peat there. If you say the name slowly, you'll see why."

Gavin tried it: "Craig — o — Moss. Craig-o-Moss. Craig of the Moss?" he asked.

"Good," said his aunt. "Always try and find out the meaning of place names. It is interesting and it can sometimes help you to identify a place if you are lost."

She went on: "From the top of Craigomas, you walk down to the glen, cross the burn and then go straight up the side of Dumyat."

Gavin peered at the brown, green and blue markings on the map. It seemed so confusing. His finger traced out the places.

"When these brown lines are far apart, it means the ground is not too steep," said Aunt Elspeth. "When they are close together, then it is steep. Look at these lines and then have a look at the hills once you are through the woods."

"There's Dumyat there," she continued. "See where the brown lines — they are called contour lines — come together, and then where the top is indicated. See, the name is marked and the height. It's over a thousand feet and you can see for miles. A few miles into the hills beyond Dumyat the peaks rise up to over two thousand feet."

"I was worried about you going off into the hills on your own," said Aunt Elspeth, "But I don't think you will go wrong today. Dumyat is easily found, and there's no mist today. You seem to have plenty of sense and I have been everywhere you are going. It is quite safe."

"Normally, it is wise to go exploring or climbing with other people," she went on "Then, if there is an accident, someone can go for help. Otherwise, if you *must* go on your own, leave a note of your route with someone else."

Gavin jotted down these points. His aunt watched him methodically stow his notebook and pencil away in the pocket of his rucksack. Gavin felt he was starting to enjoy himself. Then a thought struck him.

"Aunt Elspeth, does anyone *live* on Dumyat?"

His aunt laughed. "God bless you, no. They'd be blown off in winter. The only homes up there belong to the jackdaws. They nest in old rabbit burrows. You may see them. If you're lucky, you may see a peregrine falcon. There's one about."

"A falcon!" exclaimed Gavin. "What is it like?"

He fumbled in his pocket and drew out the bird book. He flicked over the pages until he came to an illustration of a hawk with grey back and wings, a wicked-looking hooked beak and fierce yellow eyes. Gavin read: "Inhabits lonely hills and moorland". What a find! What a bird to start his new list with! Then birds faded from his mind.

"Auntie," he exclaimed again, "would anyone climb Dumyat in the dark?"

"In the dark?" said his aunt. "No, not unless they were staying up all night to see the sunrise or were lost."

Gavin pondered for a moment. Surely people wanting to see the sunrise wouldn't climb a hill in the early evening. What *could* these lights mean?

Anyway, there was only one way to solve the mystery. Saying goodbye to his aunt, he set off down the path that led through the woods. His search for the mysterious light had begun.

4 The Falcon and the Fire

The peregrine falcon launched itself from the tiny ledge on the cliff and soared up into the blue sky. He swept round in a wide loop, his shadow passing quickly over the green and brown moorland below. His eyes scanned the ground for any movement.

Nothing stirred. The hills smiled quietly in the June sunshine. From the woods at their foot came the crooning of wood pigeons, the falcon's favourite food. But no bird flew from the trees.

Disappointed, the peregrine flew back to the ledge. It sat there motionless, except for the constant flickering of its yellow eyes as they scanned the landscape.

But the peregrine was wrong. There was someone about. Two hundred feet from the top of Dumyat, just where the grass, bracken and heather ended and the grey rocks began, there was a tiny movement in a deep clump of gorse and fern.

Gavin lay hidden. He had been there for half an hour, breathless with excitement. He was watching the peregrine. From where he lay he could look over the edge of a deep cleft in the hill. On the side facing him sat the peregrine, its dark head and grey back and barred chest showing clearly.

Gavin had seen the bird as he panted slowly to the top of the hill. Flopping to the ground, he had crawled slowly into the middle of the ferns until he was completely buried.

Slowly parting the fronds, he had peered out. It was then the peregrine began its swoop. Disappointed, Gavin lay still. He thought he had been seen. But the bird returned to its ledge.

"What a day I'm having!" thought Gavin. He lay

21

back on the soft turf and gazed at the sun through the mottled, green network of the bracken.

"It's a bit like being in the jungle," he thought. He ducked his head low and peered through the bracken stalks. There was nothing to be seen but a forest of brown trunks, with a green canopy above until it merged into a dark mass.

Gavin sighed. He did love Scotland. He had no idea there was such wild country anywhere in Britain.

His expedition had been easy so far. He had raced up the zigzag track on the front of the little hill Aunt Elspeth had called Craigomas, but by the time he got near the crest he began to pant.

He stopped on the top for a rest, enjoying the fresh smell of the grass and closely examining the gorse bushes and clumps of fern for any new birds.

Examining his map, he hurried across the flat top of the hill towards a deep wooded glen which formed a deep cleft back into the hills. He did not stop until he entered the trees which bordered both sides of a chuckling stream. A burn, they called it in Scotland. Gavin carefully picked his way across the stones, and clambered up through the trees on the other side.

Consulting his map again, he worked out that all he had to do now was to climb the slope in front of him and he would be nearly at the top of Dumyat. But when he cleared the trees, he realised that he still had a long way to go. The rocky peak of the hill still seemed blue and distant on the skyline.

"I'll take twenty steps and then halt," thought Gavin as his legs, unaccustomed to hillwalking, began to ache.

He clambered up twenty steps, paused while the ground swayed in front of his eyes, then counted another twenty. In this fashion, panting and struggling, he mounted the steep, grass slope.

The skyline grew nearer. Gavin ignored it. It would be best if he kept his head down. Still concentrating on his bursts of twenty steps, he struggled on. Suddenly, he fell forward on flat turf. He looked up. "I'm on the top," he thought with delight.

It was then that he first saw the peregrine. He immediately fell flat on his face, then crawled deep into the bracken.

Gavin's breath gradually returned. Looking around, he discovered he was not at the top of the mountain, but on a grassy shoulder leading to it.

"What now?" he thought to himself. "Where shall I start looking for the light?"

He studied the hill. It all looked so different from near the top. Down at the house, he had examined his pencil mark and had been sure he would find the exact spot. But in this world of boulders, bracken and gorse, it could have been anywhere. The higher he got, the wilder the scenery became.

Gavin came to a decision. "I'll climb to the top, then work my way down," he thought. "Even if I don't find anything, at least I will have something to tell Aunt Elspeth about."

He lurched to his feet. For the moment he had forgotten about the falcon. With a squawk, it flung itself off the cliff and soared downwards.

Entranced, Gavin watched the soaring flight. "It's like a jet plane," he thought to himself, admiring the speeding body and the cut-back streamlined wings. He watched it disappear round the side of a rocky shoulder. Then he peered more closely.

Falling down one side of the rocks was a little burn, tumbling in creamy little falls to a wide pool, then running down the hill until it disappeared in the seamed and lined lower slopes.

Beside the burn was a broad flat stretch of grass. On it, three tiny figures were seated round a fire. Gavin could see a thin thread of smoke rising up. It was too far to make out any details, but they seemed to be children.

Gavin made up his mind. He would ask their help in searching the hill for the place where he had seen the mysterious light.

He stood up. "Hi-i-i-i!" he shouted. His voice echoed back off the cliffs. Scores of jackdaws flew into the air protesting loudly.

The figures looked up, their faces small, pale dots.

Gavin waved. "Hi! Hi!" he shouted again. They *must* see him, he thought. What with the echo and the jackdaws circling noisily overhead, they must spot him.

He waved again. Then the figures moved. One minute they had been lying round their fire. The next, they were gone.

Gavin blinked. Lying on his stomach, he gazed downwards. They must have run behind the long shoulder of rock which branched off from the hill and descended in bumps and knolls to the little green valley beside the burn.

That clinched it. "They must have had something to do with the light," he thought. "Why else would they run away?"

He decided to go down to where he had last seen them. Getting to his feet, he hurried along the edge of the cliffs looking for a place to climb down.

5 The Fiery Cross

Breathless, Gavin stopped beside a tumble of huge boulders.

"It's no good," he thought. "I'll never get down there. There's nothing for it, but to go right over the crest of Dumyat and try and work my way down the other side."

He didn't really like the way to the top. All he could see ahead was a tangle of boulders as if some giant had hurled down handfuls of pebbles as big as houses. They looked pretty steep.

Picking his way carefully, he clambered slowly upwards. It was easier than he thought. He found himself enjoying the sensation of looking for the next place to put his feet. It was rather like climbing up an erratic staircase.

Soon the boulders began to be less steep and he crossed little patches of tough grass and moss. On the top of the mountain stood a small cairn, made of stones piled on top of one another. Gavin sank down beside it to get his breath back. He felt rather puffed. Still, it was all downhill after this.

Looking up, he saw a view that took his breath away. The peak of Dumyat stood at one end of the Ochil hills. At its foot were the deep woods that surrounded Uncle Fergus's house and the nearby farms.

A flat plain, dotted with farms and trees and crossed by a shining river stretched before him. On the horizon were endless rows of mountains. They seemed even bigger than the Ochils.

Gavin's eyes danced with excitement as he looked around. Why, some of the mountains were even barred with snow although it was early June. What a tale he would have to tell when he got back to the house.

He whipped his map out and tried to identify some of the hills. The Ochils stretched greenly before him. Rounded hills, broken by clefts filled with trees and singing burns with a rougher looking moorland lying beyond.

He began to study the names of some of the hills as Aunt Elspeth had suggested. What queer names. Cul Snor, White Whisp, King's Seat, Craig Leith. He tried to puzzle out their meanings, then gave up. "I'll ask Aunt Elspeth when I get back," he thought. He munched a couple of sandwiches while he sat.

Then he remembered his quest. Hurrying to his feet he began to run down the slope of the hill towards a bowl-shaped depression he had seen on the map.

Once he slipped on the grass, sliding head over heels and tearing his anorak. But speed was the thing. He had wasted enough time already.

As he trotted on, his brain worked furiously. He must get down before the fire died out. The hills were so large and confusing that he would need the smoke to find the exact spot.

Soon he found the bowl and looked over. A gentle slope covered in loose stones and sparse grass lay before him.

He hurtled downhill in great leaps in a clatter of falling stones. In no time he was at the side of the shoulder where he had seen the little valley and the figures. He stopped and listened.

Then he sniffed. He could distinctly smell burning wood. He hurried up the side of the shoulder, leaping from stones and scrambling on the grass. He was beginning to get better at hurrying on steep places.

Below him lay the little valley. Gavin gazed around warily. It was about the size of a small room, covered in smooth turf and bounded on three sides by steep rocks. Down one wall tumbled the little burn he had seen from the crest. At the open end of the valley, the burn disappeared into a grove of trees and then spilled down the hillside.

"It seems a very *secret* place," thought Gavin as he gazed around.

He wriggled forward like an Indian, until he was on the verge of the turf. No one seemed to be about. Beside the burn, the little fire still crackled and hissed, sending up its plume of smoke.

Gavin crept forward. There was no sign of life. He even leaned on the banks of the stream and looked into the brown water in case there was a hidden cave tucked away below the rocks.

Tracks! That's the thing, he thought, remembering the pictures in his book on animal tracks. They must have left tracks.

Dumping his rucksack on the ground, he began to examine the grass. Sure enough, he could see where it had been trampled and three places where it looked as if someone had been lying down. But they didn't lead anywhere.

"I must think this out carefully," Gavin decided. He took off his anorak, spread it on the grass and lay down in the sun.

He felt quite hot after all that running and climbing. He glanced at his watch. He had plenty of time before he set off for home: it was so peaceful lying in the sun, watching the reflections in the water and on the rocks.

Gavin removed his boots and socks and paddled in the cold water before sprawling once more on his anorak.

His mind turned the problem over and over. Where would a person go, who did not want to leave tracks? They had showed on the grass and in a little patch of shingle at the water's edge — and had then vanished.

Then it struck him. He gazed at the soaring grey rocks which walled in the little valley, and thought: "That's it! They climbed up the rocks. They wouldn't leave footprints there.''

Gavin was right — and wrong. The mysterious people had climbed the rocks, but regular footprints will mark even rock.

And soon he found them.

He examined a rib of rock which led up to a tangle of boulders above the pool. It seemed to be polished. It was almost as if many feet, passing that way, had worn down the rock. Here and there, there were tiny scratches.

Excited, he began to climb up. Soon he was well above the pool. He gazed down. "If I fell from here," he thought, "I'd fall right in the water."

The rocks levelled out on to a kind of platform. The scratches and smooth bumps ended in front of some moss-covered rocks. Gavin searched around in all directions. It was impossible to climb any higher. The slabs were too steep for that.

Defeated, he sat down and gazed around. He took his knife out and idly started to scrape the moss from the rock beside him. The moss came away easily. Too easily.

Gavin sat up. Quickly he scraped away more until he had cleared a space a few inches square. Underneath the moss was a large piece of wood.

Gavin, his heart pumping with excitement, did some more scraping. He uncovered more wood. It seemed to be a door covered with moss. He felt carefully around until he had identified the edges.

"I'd better not scrape off too much moss," he thought, "in case anyone comes up here." He picked up some grass and dirt from beside the rock and smeared the sections he had scraped away. That looked better.

"There must be a catch or lever here somewhere," Gavin thought. He opened the longest blade of his knife and ran it round the edges of the wood between it and the rock.

There was a slight click. The door swung open. Gavin

28

pulled it wide.

Ahead lay a dark passage. He could only see into it a few feet and then it curved sharply out of sight. It was large enough to crawl into.

Feverishly, he searched into his rucksack until he found his torch. He fastened the flex from the headpiece into the battery section and put it securely in his rucksack at the top. He adjusted the headstraps until the torch was comfortable on his forehead.

Now he was ready. He switched on. A strong beam shot from the torch and pierced the darkness. Gavin crawled into the passage. Once inside he turned round and examined the door from the inside.

Two large wooden posts were at each side of the entrance. The wooden door was fixed to it by metal hinges. It wasn't a thick door, but the front had been covered with a kind of cement into which were stuck pebbles and rock and moss until it looked just like any of the hundreds of boulders that scattered the hill.

Gavin pulled the door behind him, but made sure he knew how to open it again. It was fastened with the simple slot and lever that can be seen on any garden gate. Anyone entering simply used a thin blade like Gavin had done. It couldn't be seen from the outside. And if one knew where to insert it there would be no need to scrape away anything.

Feeling every inch a real explorer, and slightly frightened as well, Gavin crept slowly forward. Ahead of him he saw daylight. The tunnel turned sharply left into what looked like a large cave. Light was pouring in from a gash high in one corner under the rocky roof.

Gavin stood up and looked around. What had he found? He seemed to be in some kind of den or hiding place. The cave was large, big enough to hold seven or eight people standing up. It was dry and airy.

His heart thudding, Gavin looked around. On the floor lay two large skins from some brown animal. Three wooden benches stood against the wall. A long plank, set on supports, looked as if it was used as a table. Hanging on the wall was a lantern.

Beside it, on pegs, were three bows with a tin of arrows on the ground beneath. Gavin gingerly examined the bows. They were about his size, made from some kind of springy wood with strong string to shoot the arrow. The arrows had sharp points and were tipped with feathers.

Gavin could hardly believe his eyes. His feet stumbled over a box. Opening it up, he found it full of books and crockery. It was big enough to sit on.

At the back of the cave hung a large tartan blanket. It covered most of one wall. Below it on three small pegs hung three pieces of tartan cloth. Gavin examined them. They looked like sashes. Each was a different tartan. One was red, the second green and the third red with a blue and green line.

Gavin didn't know what to make of it at all. He examined everything carefully. He kept making more finds in the dim light.

In one corner was something like a round shield. It was made of wood, covered with an animal's skin and studded with iron nails. In the middle was a prong like the point of a spear. Gavin felt it. It was not very sharp.

Below the gash in the wall was a long, thick pole with little notches cut in it. Gavin could not puzzle out what these were for.

He opened up another box. Inside was a roll of tartan cloth. Opening it up carefully, he could feel something hard inside. He unrolled it slowly, but out fell the object with a clatter at his feet. Gavin picked it up. It was a knife.

But it was not an ordinary knife. It was about two feet long, with a black handle. At the end of the handle was some fine silver work clasping an orange coloured stone. The blade was sharp and shining. It had a scabbard of black leather, also covered in silver.

Gavin carefully wrapped it up again and stowed it

away in its box. He glanced at his watch. Heavens, was that the time! He would have to hurry to be home on schedule.

Making sure everything was as he had found it, he hurried back to the entrance. He listened carefully before slipping outside. The bright sun dazzled his eyes after the half-light of the cave. He sat for a moment or two until he could see again. Then he closed the door behind him and began to clamber down the rocks.

Looking back he thought to himself how well hidden the cave was. No one would know what lay behind that innocent-looking rock.

His mind full of his find, he slowly toiled his way to the top of Dumyat once more, then sped on his way back to Aunt Elspeth.

That night Gavin lay awake until very late going over every movement of his day. He had not told Aunt Elspeth anything about the cave.

He had still to find out who was using it and why. Tomorrow, he would go back, hide himself in a good spot and watch the entrance.

He fell asleep and dreamed of falcons, shining knives and high hills all mixed up together.

He was wakened by water being splashed on his face. The window was open and rain was coming in.

"That's funny," thought Gavin as he stumbled out of bed to close it. "I am sure it was closed when I fell asleep last night."

As he reached to pull down the sash, something on the sill caught his eye. He picked it up, put on the light and examined it.

It was a little cross, made of two pieces of wood tied together with string. The ends of the wood were charred. Attached to it was a shred of red tartan.

Fastened to the cross was a note. On it, printed in capital letters, was some writing.

It said: "Stay away".

6 The Hidden Watcher

Gavin awoke the next morning nearly bursting with excitement. He could feel the wooden cross beneath his pillow.

Whoever had put it on his window sill must have climbed up the ivy. That meant someone light. The ivy was not very safe. Gavin knew. He had tried it.

It must have been one of the three children he had seen. But why did they want him to stay away. Was it their cave he had found? Did the bows and boxes and the jewelled knife belong to them?

His head in a turmoil, he went downstairs for breakfast. He sat on the bottom step and pondered.

Yes, he would ask Aunt Elspeth's advice. But he wouldn't say anything about the cave yet. He pushed open the door and went in.

"You're late," said Aunt Elspeth. "Did you oversleep?"

"Yes, I did a bit," Gavin admitted. "Aunt Elspeth, can you tell me what this might be?" He laid the cross with its shred of tartan on the table. He kept the note in his pocket.

His aunt picked it up. "Well," she said, "it looks like a fiery cross. Where did you get it?"

Gavin hesitated. "I found it," he said at last. "What's a fiery cross?"

"Long ago when the chiefs of the clans wanted to call all their people together, generally to go to war, they sent a runner round all the little townships and villages. He carried a cross made of wood, and the ends were set alight. Whenever people saw the runner and the cross, they knew that they had to make their way as quickly as possible to the gathering ground. The runner didn't need to stop. Everyone knew what the sign meant. But there are no fiery crosses nowadays. It must be a game."

Gavin asked: "What's the little bit of tartan for?"

"What tartan?" said his aunt. "Oh, so there is. I didn't notice it." She examined it carefully.

"I don't know what it is for. They never attached tartan to a fiery cross in the old days. At least, I have never heard of such a thing. It's Stewart tartan," she added as an afterthought.

Gavin was interested in this business of summoning the clan. "Were there many clans?" he asked.

"Och, dozens," replied his aunt. "If you go along to your uncle's library sometime, you can look through some of his books. They'll tell you all about it. You're a member of a clan, you know."

"I am?" said the surprised Gavin.

"Yes," said Aunt Elspeth. "Your mother's name was MacRae. Your father is English, but if you ever wanted to wear a kilt you could wear the MacRae. Some of the tartan books don't like people wearing their mother's tartan, but I think it is all right."

"Do you remember the picture above the door in the library?" she continued. "Well, you'll see the MacRae tartan there. It's a fine bright shade of red! But that's enough talking for today. Eat your breakfast. What do you plan to do this morning? Would you like a packet of sandwiches and a flask?"

"Oh, yes, please," said Gavin. "I am going back up Dumyat today. I may see the peregrine again," he added carefully.

"Very well," said his aunt. "By the same route?" Gavin nodded. "And right, then, off you go," she said. "Watch yourself if you are near the cliffs. Grass can be very slippery in summer so don't go near the edges."

"Right," said Gavin.

Half an hour later, Gavin was hurrying along the woodland path to the foot of the hills. As he went, he decided on a change of plan.

"I'll have to find a different way up," he thought. "Then, if anyone is keeping a lookout for me, they won't expect me to arrive by that way."

He halted for a moment and spread his map on the ground. He thought it funny that one day's practice could turn these lines and colours and whorls into reality in his mind. He traced his journey up the Craigomas zigzag path, over the top of the hill to the glen, then up towards the top of Dumyat.

He scanned the map. Along the foot of Dumyat on one side ran a wood. A path was marked through it.

"If I go along the path," thought Gavin, "I would be hidden by the trees until I am below the bottom of the cliffs where I found the cave. That way, I could climb up from the wood. It would be easier than going to the top of the hill, then clambering down again. Besides, the only place I would be in the open would be on the slopes between the wood and the trees at the entrance to the hidden valley."

Splendid! He would be in cover practically the whole way up. He closed the map and set off.

As he entered the wood, he glanced back. He stopped, puzzled. For a moment he had thought that a man was crouching behind some trees watching him. As he looked again, he could see nothing but the green of the trees and the dark shadows beneath them. "Must be my imagination," he thought.

Then a black and white bird shot clattering out of the trees and fluttered down in a gliding flight. Gavin swung his rucksack off his shoulders, and took out his book on birds. He flicked through the illustrations.

Black and white bird, long tail, jerky flight, a kek-kek-kek cry. A picture caught his eye. A magpie! He jotted the name and date down in his notebook, then hurried on.

It was lucky seeing the magpie, he thought. He was seeing a lot of new birds. Probably he had scared it into fluttering out of the trees just then.

But Gavin was wrong. He hadn't scared the magpie.

Hidden in the trees and watching him climb up the hill was a man in dark clothing. He waited until Gavin was out of sight, then vanished in the trees.

7 The Clan Gathers

An hour later Gavin was lying hidden in a large area of fern and bracken on the edge of the rocky side of the valley. He could see the pool and the entrance to the cave.

It was very peaceful there, lying still in the warm sunshine. Then, without warning, a shadow fell across the grass in front of him.

Gavin swung round. Standing behind him was a girl of his own age and two boys, one about a year younger. All three carried bows. Each had an arrow aimed at him, Gavin noted with alarm.

The girl spoke first. "What were you doing in our cave," she said fiercely.

"I didn't know it was your cave," said Gavin. They eyed one another warily.

"We saw you spying on us," said the girl. "We don't like people following us."

"I wasn't following you," said Gavin. "I'm here on holiday and I found your cave by following the marks on the rocks."

There was a long silence while they eyed one another. Then one of the boys spoke.

"Will you promise not to tell anyone what you found?"

"Yes, I promise," said Gavin. It seemed the best thing to say with three arrows pointing at him.

"But what's your cave for? Do you play there?" he asked. The three eyed one another. Then the girl spoke again.

"We're a clan," she said. "The cave is our head-quarters."

"Oh, I'm in a clan," said Gavin, pleased at having hit on a point of friendship.

"You can't be. You're English!" said the smallest boy, speaking for the first time.

"I *am* in a clan," retorted Gavin hotly. "My aunt said so. My mother's name was MacRae. So I'm in the Clan MacRae."

The three exchanged glances again.

"Well," said the girl. "If you are in a clan, perhaps that's different." She smiled slightly. "Do you like our hats? They're called balmorals."

Gavin studied the strange hats they all wore. They were of dark blue, rather like a beret with a flat piece underneath. At the back two little dark ribbons hung down. In front was pinned a metal brooch.

"What's your badge for?" Gavin asked.

The girl took her hat off and handed it to him. The badge showed an oak leaf with a motto underneath, the whole thing surrounded by a border resembling a thick belt and buckle.

"It's the badge of the Clan Stewart," the girl said. "That's us, we're the Clan Stewart. If you have a clan, you can join us, if you like."

Gavin smiled. "What do you do?" he asked.

"Oh, we stay in our cave, practise being hunters in the hills, watch birds, cook things on fires. The clansmen of long ago could live on the hills for months. They could move silently and knew all about wild animals and birds."

"We followed you from your house this morning," she went on. "You didn't see us, but that magpie nearly gave us away."

"Yes," said Gavin. "It gave me quite a fright. I thought I saw a man in the woods as well."

"A man?" said the girl. "That's odd. So did we, but when we went to have a look there was nothing to be seen. He must have pushed off somewhere. Probably a poacher. They sometimes snare rabbits along the foot of the hill. That's why we are so careful they don't find the cave."

"It's very well hidden," said Gavin. "Where do you live?"

"We live on a farm," she said. "We pretend we live in the cave."

"It seems good fun," said Gavin. "What's your name?" he asked, after a pause.

The girl drew herself up. "My name is Clare Stewart of the Clan Stewart," she said in ringing tones. This is my brother Michael. This is my other brother Tom, but we call him Mot."

Michael chimed in: "When he was small, he tried to write his name. He was left-handed and he wrote it backwards, MOT. We still called him Mot, long after he could write TOM."

Mot grinned shyly and held out his hand. Gavin shook it, feeling slightly self-conscious.

He liked the look of the children. With their blue berets, dark anoraks and sun-burned looks, they really did look something like the clansmen in the library picture. They all had rucksacks like his, only smaller.

"Let's go down to the burn," said Clare, "and we can talk better there. It's hidden, in case there are any people climbing the hill."

She quickly picked her way down the rocks to the grass of the hidden valley. Gavin followed, admiring the neat way she climbed down.

Michael and Mot went next, their bows slung across their shoulders so they could use their hands.

"Do you hunt with the bows?" asked Gavin.

"Oh yes," said Michael. "But only rabbits. We've only hit one once, but we did kill it. We were rather sorry really."

"Clare took it home and mother took its fur off and its insides out," he continued. "Then we brought it back here and cooked it."

Mot laughed. "It took us nearly all afternoon to get a decent fire going. You see, it had been wet for days before and we had a job finding dry wood."

"Do you cook in the cave?" asked Gavin.

"No," said Clare. "The smoke might attract attention. We always cook beside the burn. The valley is well hidden, and hardly anyone sees. If they do see us, they simply think we are having a picnic. They never think there is a cave nearby."

Michael added: "Besides we try and be as secret as possible. We never leave any litter. And we always keep the turf we cut out. Look!"

He dug with his fingers at the turf. A large, square-shaped piece easily lifted up. Below was a blackened square.

"We can use stones to hem it in," said Clare. "Even when the turf is back in place, some of the scorch marks can still be seen. But only someone passing close by would see it."

"Do you sleep in the cave?" asked Gavin.

"Sometimes," said Michael. "But only when we are on holiday and during the summer. It gets very cold in winter. We never use it then."

"We take all our stuff back home," said Mot, "and hide it in our rooms until the spring."

"We're planning a snow expedition at Easter," said Clare. The Highlanders of long ago were very tough. They slept in the snow without any blankets or tents. Mother won't let us do that, but she says we can have a snow expedition with sledges if we are careful."

"Gosh," said Gavin. "That sounds fun." He was very impressed.

"Oh, it's only to the top of Ben Cleuch," said Clare. "That's the biggest hill over there. It's quite a long way away."

Gavin followed her pointing finger. He could see Ben Cleuch, a long brown shape rising above the surrounding hills.

Mot who had listened silently for a time, suddenly chimed in: "How did you find our cave?"

Clare and Michael leaned forward, intently. Feeling

he was on trial, Gavin began haltingly.

He told them of the reasons for him being on holiday, and how he had seen the light from his bedroom window.

"You clot, Mot," said Clare. "I told you someone would see it."

"Well, it wasn't my fault," said Mot indignantly. "The pole slipped. Besides, the wood isn't fitting properly."

Seeing Gavin looking mystified, he added: "We crept out of the house one night and decided to visit the cave. We've made a little wooden shutter, with grass and moss stuck on one side. It fits the gash in the roof of the cave."

Mot went on: "The shutter fits the edges of the gash exactly. But it's got a bit damp recently and the wood has warped. When we were in the cave, and had the lantern lit, the shutter came crashing down. I tried to put it up again as quickly as possible, but it crashed down again."

"Silly idiot," said Clare witheringly.

"What's the pole for?" asked Gavin, remembering the long, thick wooden pole with notches cut in it.

"Oh, that's so Mot can climb up to the shutter," said Michael. "He's the lightest. We couldn't carry anything heavier up to the cave. So we borrowed this pole from the farm and took it up one night. Clare cut notches in it with a farm saw."

Mot explained: "If I lean it against the wall, I can walk up the notches. It's a bit difficult, really. Sometimes it slips."

"He's really quite a good climber," said Clare.

"He climbed your ivy," said Michael with a grin. Mot looked bashful.

Gavin brought the cross out of his pocket. "Why did you put that on my window?" he asked.

"We thought you were spying on us," said Clare. "So we thought we would give you a fright. We didn't know you were in a clan then."

"If you want to join us, though, there are some secret things you must know," she said. "Will you swear secrecy on the Holy Iron?"

"All right," said Gavin, wondering what the Holy Iron was.

Clare reached into her rucksack and drew out the roll of tartan cloth Gavin had seen in the cave. She pulled out the jewelled knife.

"This is a Highland dagger," she said. "It's called a dirk. We found it one day in a chest in the loft."

"Long ago, the Highlanders swore oaths on the blade of their dirk," she continued. "Put your hand on the blade." Gavin did so.

"Say after me: 'I promise to keep the secrets of Clan Stewart'."

Gavin said: "I promise to keep the secrets of Clan Stewart."

"Fine," said Clare. "Now we'll explain all about the cave. Come on, let's go there."

So leaving Mot outside as a lookout — Clare was still slightly perturbed about the mysterious poacher — Gavin, Clare and Michael clambered up the rocks to the cave.

8 Back to the Cave

Clare took a small pocket-knife out of her anorak and quickly inserted it into the door catch.

"It's a bit stiff at the moment," she said. "The plaster keeps falling off and we have to renew it. Just before you came we had finished it off and it looked quite good. We found that real moss was growing on it in some places."

She pulled the door open and crawled in. Gavin and Michael followed her.

"Pull the door behind you," said Clare. "Mot can open it himself."

For the second time in two days Gavin found himself crawling along the short passageway.

"Have you a torch?" asked Clare. Gavin brought his head-torch out of his rucksack.

"Put it on," said Clare. "My batteries are running low."

Gavin dutifully switched on. Michael also produced a small torch.

They entered the cave, the light beams sweeping round and glinting on the boxes and the shield on the wall, throwing the red tartan cloth into sharp relief.

"Sit down," said Clare, "and I'll tell you about the cave."

"How did you find it?" asked Gavin.

"It's an old silver mine," Michael chimed in. "We were playing up here one day and saw the opening. So we ran home for candles and then crawled in."

"We were a bit afraid," said Clare. "A lot of the rock on Dumyat is not very safe. It's called pudding-stone."

She went across to one wall, kicked a few splinters off a protruding rock, and passed them to Gavin.

He examined them. They were just like rounded puddings stuck together. He glanced nervously at the roof.

"It's all right," said Michael. "There's only one patch beside that wall that is loose. The rest is quite firm."

Clare flashed her torch on the wall, then turned the beam on Michael.

"Give Mot a shout and we'll take down the shutter. It's silly to waste batteries."

Michael obediently set off for the entrance.

"The climbing pole is a bit thin for Michael and me," said Clare, after Michael had disappeared. "We leave the shutter in place because some rain can blow in. Jackdaws and pigeons would also get inside and make a mess."

In a few minutes Michael was back with the grinning Mot.

"There's no one around," said Mot, getting to his feet and dusting himself.

"Open the shutter, Mot," commanded Clare.

Gavin watched with interest as Mot went to one wall, picked up a long pole and set it against the wall below the gash he had seen when he first entered the cave.

Very carefully, Mot began to climb up, placing his feet slowly in the cut-slots. Soon he was above their heads.

"Hold the pole steady," he shouted down. Clare and Michael held it on either side. Mot reached up and detached the shutter. He lowered it carefully on an attached rope to the floor of the cave. Light flooded in, making Gavin blink. They all switched off their torches.

"We found the cave last year," said Clare. "It was made to mine silver and goes much further into the hill. But it has been blocked up. Look!"

She pulled aside the tartan cloth. Behind it was a heap of piled boulders and rubble.

"We tried to move a lot of it to get in," said Michael.

"But there's too much of it. So we just covered it up."

"When we got inside the main entrance," said Clare, "we found that there were two wooden posts at each side. We don't know what they were for. Perhaps the miners had a little door to keep sheep out when they were away."

"Anyway," she went on, "we asked Dad for some old wood and we made a door to fit."

"Dad gave us some hinges and a catch," said Michael, "but we didn't tell him exactly what it was for. He just asked us to be careful."

"It took us a day to carry the door up here and to fit it up," added Mot. "The plaster was the worst part."

"We tried everything," said Michael.

"It kept falling off," said Clare. "But in the end we bought some outdoor glue-solution that Dad uses on farm buildings. We mixed that with the plaster and coated the door with it. We painted it like the rock and then stuck moss and lichen into it. When it is freshly done, it looks very like a real rock."

"I know," said Gavin. "I only found it by accident. I didn't know where you had gone and I was simply scraping at the rock to pass the time."

"The weather affects it," said Clare. "But if we keep repairing the camouflage, no one will ever find it."

She looked affectionately round the cave. "I bet no one has ever had such a good hideout," she said with satisfaction.

"Have you shown Gavin the marks," said Mot.

"What marks?" asked Gavin.

Clare stood up and pointed to one wall. There were patches of red stone seaming the grey rocks and sections of white quartz. Every now and again there were smooth scorings about an inch wide and a foot long.

"We think these are dynamite markings," said Clare. "The mine is hundreds of years old, but later miners tried to widen it to see if the silver had all been dug out. Dad says it has all gone now."

She sat down on one of the wooden benches. "Sit down," she said to Gavin. "It's silly to stand."

Mot and Michael took off their bows and hung them on the pegs driven into cracks in the wall.

Gavin also sat down. "Did you make the seats?" he asked.

"Yes," said Clare. "Dad gave us some old wood and we brought it up here. Michael and Mot hammered them together to make the seats and the table. It can get slightly damp if there is a lot of rain so we keep everything in tin boxes."

"That's one of the reasons we made the shutter for the gash," she went on. "It stops anyone seeing our light if we are here in the dark, and it keeps the wet out when we are away."

Gavin sat back on his seat with a feeling of pleasure. It *was* fun to be sitting in a hidden cave talking to his new friends.

"What are the sashes for?" he said, pointing to the wall.

"Oh, these are the three tartans of the Clan Stewart," said Clare. She handed them over to Gavin.

"The red one is Royal Stewart, the tartan worn by the pipers in the Highland regiments. The green one is Hunting Stewart, a tartan worn for hunting. It can't be seen easily. The last one is Stewart of Appin, one of the main branches of the Clan. We only wear them on important occasions. There are some other Stewart tartans but we've missed them out."

"What does the Clan do?" asked Gavin.

Clare glanced at Mot and Michael. "You said he could join," said Michael.

"He'll have to take the oath," said Mot.

"But I took the oath," said Gavin. "I swore on the Holy Iron."

"That was just to see the cave," said Clare. "To join the Clan, you must go through the full ceremony of allegiance. But I suppose I can tell you a little. We try and find out about Scottish history..."

Gavin's face fell. History! How dull!

Clare saw his look and said hurriedly: "But we make it good fun. We play at being clansmen and we try and teach ourselves to live on the hills and in the woods in all weathers and to move silently like wild animals."

"And to watch birds and keep diaries and notebooks about them," said Mot.

"Oh, I'm interested in birds," said Gavin.

Mot looked pleased. He opened a tin box beside him.

"We keep a list of the birds we've seen. So far, we've seen eighty-eight different species."

Gavin gasped. Eighty-eight! Why he had only seen about twenty so far. He studied the notebook Mot gave him, his eyes running down the names. Buzzards ... herons ... three kinds of owls ... sparrow-hawk ... oyster-catcher ... birds he had never heard of.

"I saw a peregrine," he said.

"Yes," said Mot, "it nests on Craig Leith, the large hill with the crag at the top."

"Yes, I remember it," said Gavin.

"We do other things as well," said Michael. "Soon Dad is going to teach us how to be proper mountaineers and how to climb in the winter."

"We picnic and swim in the pool in the hidden valley," said Clare. "We build huts in the woods and light fires and cook on them. And we explore the Ochils as much as we can."

It sounded fun, Gavin thought. Birds, huts, cooking on fires and exploring.

He remembered something one of the others had said. "And you don't cook at all in the cave?" he asked.

"No," said Clare. "We found the smoke could be seen pouring out of the gash and it smelled the cave. So we just cook in the hidden valley."

"Aunt Elspeth has a primus stove," said Gavin, remembering that he had seen one in her kitchen cupboard. "I could perhaps borrow that and you could cook a meal in the cave."

Mot and Michael were visibly impressed.

"That's great!" said Clare. "We can have a Clan Council for your oath of allegiance and then we can have a feast afterwards."

"Good," said Gavin. "Well, that's settled."

"There's just one thing," said Clare. "You'll have to pass an initiative test first."

9 Testing Time

"A *what* test?" asked Gavin.

"An initiative test," repeated Clare. "When our cousin Freda wanted to join the Clan we made her hunt and shoot a rabbit with a bow and arrow and then cook it."

"Did she do it?" asked Gavin.

"Yes," said Clare. "But we all helped in the end. We only killed one rabbit. We felt so sorry for it that we didn't kill any more."

"Mot's got a hat made of rabbit skins," said Michael. "It looks like an Eskimo hat. In fact, he tries to tell people that the Eskimos gave it to an uncle who is a ship's captain and the uncle gave it to him. Actually, he got the skins from Dad."

Mot coloured. "It is an Eskimo hat," he said stoutly. "The Eskimos did give it away."

"I'm not surprised they gave it away," said Clare. "You should smell it."

Gavin returned to the question of the initiative test. "What would you like me to do?" he asked.

Clare thought for a moment. Then she slapped her thigh with one hand.

"I've got it," she said. "You can be a fugitive and we'll hunt you down. If we catch you, you can't join. If you stay free, we'll make you a member of the Clan Alliance."

Gavin blinked. A fugitive? It sounded rather a hard test.

Clare spread a map on the floor. "Gather round," she said. Mot, Michael and Gavin knelt down and peered at the map.

Clare traced a wide circle with her finger. "Do you see this area here," she said, her finger marking out the whole of Dumyat, the woods at the base, Aunt Elspeth's house and large grounds and the three nearest hills.

"Well, you have a day and a night to find or build yourself a hideout," Clave went on. You must cook one meal in it and sleep one night in it. We'll try and track you down."

Gavin thought hard. He looked at the map again. It certainly seemed a very wide area, thick with woods and containing a lot of wild country. Surely he could find somewhere to hide.

"Do you think that's fair, Clare?" said Michael. "After all, Gavin is new to this area. Should we not give him an extra day to do his planning, then hunt for him."

Mot chimed in. "Yes," he added. "Besides, Gavin is from the city. He doesn't know anything about lighting a fire out of doors, what wood to choose and so on."

"Let him have one day to prepare," he continued. "I'll teach him something about the different trees in the meantime. What do you say, Gavin?"

Gavin thought. It did seem to be a bit better if Mot was going to show him the ropes.

"All right," he said. "That's fine by me."

"Good," said Clare. "Now let's go over it again. Today is Tuesday. Gavin can have the rest of today to plan, if he likes. Mot can teach him some woodcraft tomorrow, Wednesday. But from Thursday morning, all through Thursday until Friday night, he's a fugitive."

"If we don't catch Gavin, where shall we meet when the contest is over?" asked Michael.

"We'd better meet in the cave. We'll make it at night, so that Gavin has plenty of time to get back to his house if he is making his hideout far away. Is that agreed?"

"Agreed!" chorused Mot and Michael.

"Agreed," said Gavin, who had little choice.

"Great," said Clare. "We can really have some fun. And we'll make a Clan feast the next night. If you win through, Gavin, we'll make you the Clan scout.''

"I'm the Chief," Clare went on. "Mot is the sword-bearer — he carries our dirk at council meetings. Michael is the clan piper. Actually, he doesn't play the pipes. But he's got a mouth-organ. He only knows three tunes. A march, a dance tune and a lament.''

"What's a lament?" asked Gavin.

"It's a sad tune played when someone dies, generally someone famous, a hero or something like that.''

"What are the tunes called?" asked Gavin, who quite liked music.

"The march is 'Hielan' Laddie'," said Michael, pulling a mouth-organ out of his pocket and playing a few bars of a stirring marching tune. "The dance tune is 'Kate Dalrymple'." With more confidence, he played a lively tune with a quick beat that made Gavin want to tap his feet.

"The lament is 'Lochaber No More'," continued Michael. Getting slightly red in the face with effort, he played a slow, mournful tune that seemed very tuneless to Gavin. Out of breath, Michael returned the mouth organ to his pocket.

"He only knows three," said Clare again, this time in a tone of disgust.

"I'm practising a fourth," said Michael.

"What is it?" asked Gavin.

"Lament for Clare Stewart," retorted Michael.

A few minutes later, Gavin was bounding down the hill.

He must make haste. He wanted to question Aunt Elspeth about the estate: she might know some good hiding places unknown to the Clan.

After all, it was a private estate. Even the daring members of the Clan would not go there as often as they did on to the hills. That seemed the best bet.

He hurried on, his mind full of plans for hideouts. Anyway, he did have some time to prepare. He would spend the evening planning his campaign.

Tomorrow morning, Mot was going to teach him woodcraft. After that, he was on his own.

10 The Secret Castle

Gavin raced into the house, burst in through the front door and took the stairs two at a time up to his bedroom. Breathless, he dumped his anorak and rucksack on the floor of his room, then bounded downstairs again to the kitchen.

His aunt looked at him in surprise. "What on earth's the hurry?" she asked.

"Aunt," gasped Gavin. "I need some advice."

"Well, you can have my advice while you are eating your tea," retorted his aunt, pulling out a chair from the table. "Now, not another word until you are eating."

Seeing she was being quite firm, Gavin dutifully sat down and began to chew quickly. He swallowed a few mouthfuls, then said anxiously:

"Aunt Elspeth, do you know any good hiding places on the estate?"

"Hiding places?" said his aunt in surprise. "What kind of hiding places?"

Quickly Gavin told her about meeting his new friends. He said nothing about having to sleep in his hiding place: just that he was to be a fugitive and the Clan would try and hunt him down.

His aunt's lips twitched. "I know your Clan," she said. "Clare's father is a friend of your Uncle Fergus. He sometimes comes over here, but he hasn't been for some time — since your uncle began working so hard on his book."

"You seem to have met some nice friends," she went on. "So you need somewhere you can hide for a day and cook a meal. That's not too easy. I tell you what. You carry on with your tea and I'll slip into the library and get the estate map off the wall. We can have a look at that."

So, with a reassuring pat on the shoulder, she left the room. A few minutes later, she returned carrying a large map in a glass case.

"Phew," she said. "The back is covered with dust. Give me a hand to clear the table."

Gavin eagerly jumped down and hurried over to the draining-board beside the sink, and fetched and carried plates and cups until the large table was cleared. His aunt put the map down and looked at it carefully.

"When Uncle Fergus's grandfather was alive," she said, "the estate was much bigger than it is today. The family made a lot of money out of jute mills in Dundee, and they bought this estate and developed it."

"Do you remember the stone wall bordering the drive and the old lodge at the gates and the pillars with the lions on top?" she continued. Gavin nodded. "Well, they built all that. They came here to hunt and fish and relax in the days when there were plenty of wealthy landowners. There are not so many today."

She chuckled. "Your Uncle Fergus and I are certainly not rich, but the estate is still quite big. Some of the silver he is so proud about came from his grandfather."

"I remember when I was a girl we used to walk along some of the estate paths to summer houses that were built in the woods. Some of them were falling into disuse and the paths were getting overgrown. There was one that might suit you. It was built to look like a hidden castle."

"A castle?" asked Gavin, in disbelief.

"Yes," said his aunt. "It was built as a summer playground for children. But it had got a bit derelict when we visited it. I remember the path passed at the foot of a cliff and just beside two yew trees. You should be able to find them. Yes, here it is."

"What are yew trees?" said Gavin, following her finger on the map.

"They are evergreens. There aren't many here, so you should find them in the wood. They will be thick and dark green and there are only two of them. That wood is nearly all plane and beech trees and their leaves will be light green."

"Now take a look at this," his aunt went on. "Do you see that path branching off near the house? It runs past the old ornamental loch down to a narrow road through the woods. The road is still used by farm carts and forestry workers. The path crosses the road and goes back into the woods again through an old gateway. You'll find that the path is still well trodden as far as that. It then runs up through the woods to the cliffs at the top, just before the woods finish at the foot of the hills. But the path after that will be overgrown. You might find that the castle has tumbled down. But it's worth a look. It had a fireplace. When you said you had to cook a meal, that's what brought it back to me."

"Thanks, Aunt Elspeth, that sounds fine," said Gavin. "Do you think the Stewarts know of it?"

"No, I'm sure they don't," said his aunt. "You see, most of their time, I gather, is spent on the Ochils. Or so their father says. They do come into these woods, but the woods are supposed to be private. I know they do come in — and I don't mind — but I'm sure they don't come in very often. Anyway, you'll have time this evening to go and have a look. You'll be able to see if there are any tracks to tell you if they have been there."

"Yes, I'll go now," said Gavin, getting to his feet. "Thanks a lot, Aunt Elspeth."

"Oh, that's all right," she said. "We must uphold the honour of the MacRaes!"

Encouraged by this last remark, Gavin made another request. "Auntie, if I gave you most of my pocket money would you buy me three things in Stirling?"

"Certainly," said his aunt. "What are they?"

"I'd like a blue balmoral bonnet, with ribbons at the back, a MacRae badge, and a sash of MacRae tartan.

That's what all the Stewarts have, but theirs is Stewart tartan, of course. You see, if I win and stay hidden, I can join the Clan Alliance."

Aunt Elspeth laughed again. She seemed to be enjoying this as much as Gavin.

"All right," she said. "I planned to go into Stirling on Thursday. In fact, I was going to stay overnight and return here on Friday morning. I sometimes do that when I go to visit on old school friend. She's ill, you see, and likes company. It would only be for one night, or two at the most. I've told Uncle Fergus to leave his silver notes for once, and devote his time to you."

"Oh, I don't want to disturb him," said Gavin. "I shall really be quite all right by myself."

"It'll do him good," said Aunt Elspeth. "He needs disturbing. Off you go and see if you can find the two yew trees and the castle. But be sure and be back by bedtime."

Gavin was soon hurrying through the woods, enjoying the sensation of having no rucksack on his back.

What a holiday I'm having," he thought. It seemed to have been excitement since he first arrived. Tomorrow Mot was going to teach him how to crawl and stalk animals and how to light woodland fires.

Soon he had trotted down to the sunken road that Aunt Elspeth had mentioned. He searched along the stone wall bordering it until he found the narrow entrance between the pillars. There was no gate, only moss-covered steps and the pillars now green and chipped by the weather.

He stopped and looked ahead. The evening sun was slanting down through the tall trees, throwing their light green leaves into sharp relief.

He listened carefully and looked around. One could never tell. Perhaps the Clan was hunting him already. But there was no sound, only the singing and whistling of the evening birds and the soft swishing noise that comes when trees are moving softly in the wind.

The path was covered in dead leaves, but Gavin could see its outline quite clearly. It curved up the slope until it disappeared in huge clumps of rhododendrons and other bushes. The ground was carpeted with ferns and coarse grass and other woodland plants.

Soon the ground grew steep and the slope became slippery. Gavin had to cling to the boles of trees to pull himself up. He stopped breathless, leaning against the smooth trunk of a tall ash. There was no path now, just a steep slope closely covered with trees and bushes.

He pushed his way upwards, noisily crushing dead branches and twigs underfoot. Branches whipped against his anorak and face as he tried to find open spaces. He came across a little clearing and sat down to plan his next move.

All around he could see nothing but trees and green undergrowth. Nothing stirred. Even the birds had fallen silent. There was still plenty of light, but the shadows were lengthening as the sun went down.

What was it Aunt Elspeth had said? Look for the dark green mass of two yews. You can see it against the light green of other trees. That was it.

Gavin carefully examined the ground ahead. Peeping out from among the trees he could see a large cliff, with more trees at its top, and brambles and other creepers growing on its face.

He struggled up to the foot of the cliff. It did seem as if the ground was flat there. It could perhaps have been a path once. Picking his way carefully he moved slowly along the foot of the rock. Glancing upwards, he could not see the top because the trees and bushes hung well over.

Then, rounding a corner, he came across a little stone arch. From a distance, it could not be seen. It just looked like any number of grey-barked trees in the woods. It rose from one side of the path and curved up and over until it merged into the cliff. At its far side, the ground fell away in another tumble of rocks.

Through the arch, Gavin could see two dark trees. Excited, he moved forward. The path was firm and free from branches, although it had a layer of brown, dead leaves. The cliff on his right was sheer and smooth.

On his left were the two yew trees, old and thick and dark. They formed an impenetrable mass beside the path. Gavin stopped to examine the wood of their cork-like trunks, and the dark green needles. The yews effectively hid the stone arch from below. The cliff and the overhanging trees hid it from above.

Then, suddenly, he was in the middle of the castle. The path ended in a grassy glade about the size of a small room. A chest-high stone wall ran along the left of the path, ending in a tower built against the back of the cliff.

When Gavin peered over he could only see the tops of trees waving greenly below him. If he reached out he could touch the top twigs. He guessed that they must hide the castle from below.

Built against the cliff in a corner was a chimney of grey stone with an open space at its foot. Smoke from the fire would be hidden until it merged at the top of the cliff and would then be lost in the branches of the trees at the top. Even if someone saw the smoke and looked down they would not be able to see where it was coming from.

But the most exciting part was still to come. A staircase ran up the side of the cliff. It was bordered by a stone wall on the left. Gavin mounted it slowly, kicking and scraping at the dead leaves and twigs that hid the stone steps. The steps ended at the top of the tower which formed the far part of the castle.

From the top Gavin could look over the top branches of the trees. Beyond he could see the silver water of the Forth river and the houses of Stirling, with the castle on its rock behind. He felt just like a bird. It was just as though he, too, were perched on a top twig. What a place!

Looking down from the tower, he could see that the walls at the front of the little castle were really quite high, and they were built of the same stone as the cliff behind. From quite close up, they would appear to be the cliff.

The only entrance — and exit — was through the archway that Gavin had first discovered. No one could climb the cliffs from below and no one could climb up the cliffs from the floor of the castle.

Peering down, he could see that there was another small room at the foot of the door, on the edge of the green space, but the walls had tumbled down. None of the rooms had roofs. There was nowhere covered in. But it was still a splendid hiding place.

Gavin clambered down with a sigh of satisfaction. He now had a secret den. And he also had a plan to put the hounds off the scent.

11 Lessons in the Woods

Gavin and Mot sat side by side on a log in the Bluebell Wood. Mot was talking. Gavin was listening intently, occasionally making notes in his red notebook.

"First of all," said Mot, "have you done any stalking or playing at Indians in the woods?"

"No," said Gavin sadly.

"All right," said Mot. "Then watch me. The first thing to remember is that any movement catches the eye. So, if you are moving through trees and are caught in a clearing or opening, don't try and leap quickly into cover. Freeze where you are. The chances are that you won't be seen."

He pointed along a path to a clump of tall elm trees. "Do you see these trees? I'll go over to them and hide somewhere near them. Try and spot me. I'll whistle when I am ready. In the meantime, turn your back."

Gavin obediently turned round on the log. A few minutes later came the whistle. He swung round quickly, his eyes searching the trees and bushes for any sign of Mot. There was nothing, just a mass of green and brown as the trees interlaced with one another.

"Okay," he shouted. "I give up."

Mot emerged from behind some bushes, grinning broadly. "Now watch this," he said. "When I whistle you turn round. Then I'll move quickly. See if you can see me this time."

Again, Gavin turned round. Again came the whistle. Again Gavin scanned the trees. Then a quick movement caught his eye. His head swivelled round. When he looked carefully he could see Mot outlined against the bushes.

"Got you!" he shouted. "Try moving again, then stop."

Mot moved quickly, then froze. When he moved Gavin saw him. When he stopped, he merged with the forest.

"Come out, I'm satisfied," shouted Gavin. Mot joined Gavin on the log again.

"You see," he said. "There's nothing to it. There are some other things you should remember. Don't wear bright colours. You will be all right with your green anorak. Try and get against a dark background. Don't show yourself against the skyline. You can be seen easily that way."

Gavin wrote these points down.

"Anything else you want ask me?" said Mot.

"Yes," said Gavin. "How do you move silently in the woods?"

"The main thing to remember is to move slowly," said Mot, getting up from the log. "You examine the ground ahead for a dozen yards or so, then examine the woods or moorland in front of you to make sure the animal or bird you are watching hasn't seen you."

"You then put your foot down very slowly, walking only on the sole," continued Mot. "Keep your heels up. Look out for dried twigs or branches that might snap or crackle. In some places where there are lots of dried leaves it is impossible to move quietly, so try and avoid these places. Now watch me."

Slowly he examined the ground between him and a large oak tree twelve or thirteen feet away. Then he searched the trees and bushes beyond. Then, one foot slowly in front of the other, he moved over the ground with hardly a sound. Twice he stopped to silently avoid overhanging branches and the clutching ends of bushes.

Then Gavin tried it. For the first few feet he was fairly successful. Then, in trying to avoid the bushes, he stepped on a dead branch. It snapped with a loud crack. A blackbird fluttered, shrieking, out of nearby bushes.

Mot laughed. "It's harder than I thought," said Gavin.

"It will come with practice," said Mot comfortingly.

"I know," said Gavin. "But I haven't time to practise. I'm on my own from tomorrow night. Hold on a minute while I write all these points down."

Gavin jotted down: — examine the background.
— examine the ground.
— move on the ball of the foot.
— watch out for dried twigs and branches.
— freeze if caught in an open space.
— wear dark clothes.
— don't be seen against the skyline.

Well, that's that, he thought. It should be a help.

"Now, there are one or two other things," said Mot. "Do you know how to stalk or crawl?" Gavin shook his head.

"Watch me," said Mot.

He lay down on the ground, then slowly wriggled forward using the fore part of his arms to lever himself up slightly, then moved each leg carefully and silently forward. In a series of slightly jerky but entirely silent movements he moved forward.

"Now you try it," he said to Gavin.

Gavin jumped off his log and lay down on the grass and undergrowth. He wriggled forward. At first it was tiring and he kept dragging his legs instead of lifting them up and setting them down quietly. When he glanced back he had scraped a path through the undergrowth, whereas Mot had left no sign.

He practised by himself for a time while Mot perched on the log and commented on his progress. Eventually, Mot said he was satisfied.

"There are some camouflage rules you should remember," said Mot. "Keep watching me."

He left Gavin and darted forward towards a rise in the ground covered in large ferns. He disappeared into them. Gavin watched intently. Then he saw Mot's face, looking like a pale disc among the green stalks and fronds of the ferns.

Mot came trotting towards him. "You saw my face?" he asked. Gavin nodded. "Watch me this time," said Mot disappearing into the ferns again.

Gavin examined the ferns, but there was no sign of Mot's face this time. Then the ferns rustled and swayed and Mot stood up.

"Come here," he shouted. Gavin went towards him. Mot presented a strange sight. He had smeared his face with dirt and had stuck ferns inside the collar of his anorak so that fronds half-covered his face.

Gavin laughed. Mot grinned as well, his teeth shining whitely in his darkened face.

"Remember that if you are hiding, the most easily seen part of you is your face. It really looks quite white from a distance."

"I'll remember," said Gavin.

Mot looked at him, grinning. "Haven't you forgotten something?" he asked.

"What?"

"To write it down in your notebook!" Gavin grinned bashfully, then dutifully added the point about white faces to his growing list of stalking notes.

"Is there anything else I should know?" he asked.

Mot thought for a moment then said: "The most important thing is what I said about movement." Gavin wrote busily.

"If you are stalking anybody or a bird or animal," said Mot, "and if you want to look at them when lying down, remember and raise your head very slowly inch by inch. No jerky movements. And bring your head down in the same way. Got that? All right, then let's see you trying it again."

So Gavin happily smeared his face with dirt, and under the expert eye of Mot, practised walking silently, then crawling, until he began to feel that he was truly part of woodland life.

12   In the Valley

"Come here," whispered Mot. Gavin crawled up beside him.

Mot pointed through the trees that lined the entrance to the hidden valley. Clare and Michael were lying flat beside a pool, their sleeves rolled up to the shoulder and their hands buried deep in the water. Both lay motionless.

"What are they doing?" asked Gavin.

"They're guddling trout," said Mot. Gavin looked blank.

"They're trying to catch trout with their hands," said Mot. "The trout lie close beside the bank when the weather is hot. The water is quite deep there and they like to lie in the shadows."

"Why don't they swim away when they see the hands?" asked Gavin.

"They don't notice if you do it very slowly," said Mot. "You wriggle your fingers round about them. They think it is just the motion of the water or reeds swirling ... or something. Anyway, they never move. But it's got to be done very slowly and quietly. Watch and you'll see."

Gavin watched with interest, admiring the scene of the sunlit valley with its green floor and high grey rocky sides. Then he gasped.

In one quick movement, Clare twisted sideways. Something arched through the air and flopped on the grass. She raced across to it, a stone in hand. She gave the fish a wallop on the head.

Michael stood up from his side. "It's no good now, Clare," he said. "You've scared them."

"Well, we've got five," retorted Clare. "That's enough. Besides, we've been at it for hours."

She swung round as Mot emerged from the trees, accompanied by Gavin. "Hello, Gavin," she shouted. "Come and see this."

Gavin looked at the line of small trout lying at her feet. They looked very small, with their slim lines and freckled backs.

"How do you cook them?" he asked at last.

"Come on and I'll show you," she said, leading the way to a smooth stretch of turf near the grove of trees.

Clare started to organise lunch. "Mot, you cut out the fireplace. Michael, you go with Gavin and collect wood. I'll clean the trout." Obediently, Mot took out his knife and started to cut a square in the turf.

Michael led Gavin towards the trees. Gavin watched closely as Michael started to collect wood. He only went to certain trees, Gavin noticed.

First of all, he broke off any long, thin dead twigs and piled them up on the ground. Then he made another pile of dead moss, withered ferns and pieces of bark. Gavin turned to help, picking up twigs from the ground.

"Hey, don't do that," said Michael.

"Do what?" said Gavin.

"Pick them off the ground. They're always damp. Once we've got the fire going we can use wood picked up from the ground. But to get it started the wood has to be absolutely dry. And you need to pick certain trees. Make a pile of these bigger bits because Clare will need lots of wood."

Michael took off his anorak and laid it on the ground. Then he piled all his small pieces of wood, the dead ferns and chunks of bark into it and knotted the sleeves together.

"Bring these bigger pieces, Gavin," he said.

Gavin quickly took off his anorak and piled the long twigs and bigger logs on to it. He cradled his load in his arms and followed Michael back to the grass beside the stream.

Mot had cut out a square of turf and had set it safely

to one side. Then he ringed two of the sides of the square with flat stones.

"Get your notebook out, Gavin," he said with a smile. "Here's another lesson for you. You'll need it tomorrow when you're on your own."

So Gavin squatted down on his heels and watched Mot closely.

First of all, Mot placed a tiny "Y" shaped twig in the middle of the square with the stem pushed into the ground. Then he grouped the ferns, small twigs and flakes of bark round about it.

Very carefully, he broke up some of the long thin twigs and laid them on top of the "V" of the stick, building them round until he had something resembling a little, wooden Indian tepee. He kept a gap on one side.

He kept shouting out remarks to Gavin who tried to get them down in his book. "Never light a fire in the middle of a wood or near a wood, Gavin — in the summer the undergrowth can get tinder dry. Stay away from plantations, firwoods and any trees like that."

He snapped some more sticks. "They've got resin in them you know — a kind of wood oil," he went on. "It flares up. Twigs like that are fine for kindling a fire though, but light your fire well away from woods or plantations or dry moorland."

Snap. Crack. Snap. "Can you tell different kinds of trees?" asked Mot. Gavin shook his head.

Clare looked up from where she was sorting out some tin plates. "I'll give you a book we've got in the cave. That'll help. I'll mark the different trees for you. Pass me that frying pan, Michael."

She began to spread cooking fat over the bottom of the pan. "Will you be long, Mot?"

"No," said Mot. "Here goes. Bring me some of that larger wood, Gavin, and pile it over here."

He leaned over the little pyramid of wood, took a box of matches out of his pocket and laid two on the ground. "We only allow ourselves two," he told Gavin.

"Any more and Clare gives us a punishment."

"She made me run to the top of Dumyat and back," Michael said ruefully.

"Gosh," thought Gavin. "Only two matches. Suppose the wood were damp. Suppose the wind blew the matches out."

"It is easy after a bit of practice," said Clare.

Mot leaned carefully over the fire, and shielding the match with the cup of his hand he struck one and applied the spurting flame to the kindling wood. Puffs of blue smoke eddied upwards, then thickened and billowed in the still summer air.

Little flames flared up. The larger sticks began to crackle. Everybody cheered, including Gavin. Mot put the spare match back in his box with a nonchalant air.

There was a smell of woodsmoke, a smell that was to recall his holiday adventure for Gavin whenever he smelled it in the future. Soon the flames were roaring up from the fire.

"Put the big stuff on," said Michael. Gavin carefully laid some of the bigger pieces on the flames. The heat dropped a little as the flames curled round their new fuel.

Meanwhile, Clare was laying the trout in the grease of the pan. She placed the pan over the flames. There came a sound of sizzling. The Clan sat round the fire, gloating.

"Oh, boy," thought Gavin to himself. "This *is* fun, cooking in the open air like this. I wonder when I'll learn to be as expert out of doors as Clare or Mot."

Soon Clare pronounced the meal ready. Mot poured some water on the fire and clouds of grey-white smoke billowed out. There was a hissing from the stones and charred wood.

Michael handed round the tin plates. There was one whole trout and a piece each. Gavin looked round for cutlery.

"There's none, I'm afraid," said Clare, anticipating

his glance. "We took it home from the cave and forgot to bring it back. Use your knife."

She pulled out her knife and expertly slit the skin from the trout and drew out the backbone. Gavin copied her.

The fish was very hot, but delicious. He quickly polished off his portions and followed it with two apples provided by Mot.

Digging into his rucksack, he produced some cheese and a packet of biscuits Aunt Elspeth had given him. He handed these round. The Clan ate steadily, in a blissful silence.

Afterwards they lay on their backs in the sun and chatted. Gavin told them about his home in London and why he had come to Scotland on holiday. Clare told him about their farm, and about their adventures. Mot and Michael chimed in from time to time.

They were pleased Gavin knew something about birds, and produced diaries from the cave and a book of feathers for his inspection. He liked the feathers book. It seemed much more sensible than collecting eggs which only faded after a time and distressed the mother bird when they were taken.

The boys had stuck feathers from birds they had found dead, or feathers they found in the moulting season, into an album. Beside each feather they had pasted bird pictures clipped from magazines, and had written in the date, place and a description of the bird's habits. Gavin found it fascinating and vowed to start his own book.

They then had a shooting match with the bows and arrows, sticking a tin plate in the grass and firing at it. The afternoon passed in a sunny haze.

The sun was starting to go down when Gavin said goodbye to the Clan.

Clare gave him a small book. "It's a book on trees. I've marked each tree with a cross if the wood is good for kindling. I've put a tick if it is good for steady burning. You'll be surprised what you'll learn in two days on your own."

Gavin thanked her politely, privately wondering how he was going to remember all he had been told already.

Mot pushed a bundle of leaves into his rucksack. "What are these?" asked Gavin.

"Samples," said Mot. "They'll help you identify the trees."

Clare ended the conversation. "We'll have to hurry. Gavin will have to leave soon. So let's tidy up first, then we'll go over the rules for Gavin's initiative test."

Mot took the remainder of the unused wood and tucked it away out of sight beneath a handy stone.

Michael tossed the stones back into the bracken and into the stream. He scraped out the charred cinders and threw them into the burn below the trees where they were quickly carried out of sight downstream. Then he replaced the square of turf.

Clare wandered around packing up. She picked up all scraps of paper. In a trice all signs of a Clan feast had vanished.

"Right!" she said, briskly. "From first light tomorrow morning Gavin is on his own. He has to find a hideout, spend one night in it and cook one meal in it. He needn't stay longer than that in the actual hideout, but he has got to stay uncaught."

"If Gavin is not caught, then we'll all meet in the cave by midnight," Clare went on. "Is that agreed?" They all nodded. "You've got a wide area to hide in, Gavin, but we know the area so odds are on our side. If you're still free by midnight tomorrow night, you can join the Clan Alliance. Does that sound fair to you?"

Mot and Michael regarded Gavin gravely.

"Yes," said Gavin. "That's fine."

He grinned. "Well," he said. "Good hunting!" He smiled again. "See you in the cave!"

Clare snorted. "Don't worry, we'll catch you," she

said. She raised her hand in an ancient salute of farewell.

As Gavin trotted down towards the Bluebell Wood and the path home, he allowed himself one glance back.

He could see three heads on the skyline, the feathers on their balmorals silhouetted against the reds and yellows of the setting sun. This time no hands were raised in farewell.

The hounds were getting ready for the chase.

13   Hounds on the Scent

An owl's hoot rang through the wood. It was not the "hoo-hoo-hoo" that outlaws in Robin Hood films were apt to use. It was the shrieking "ki-wick" of the tawny owl.

The Clan knew its business.

Mot put his hands to his mouth ... and another "ki-wick" resounded through the darkened trees. A figure emerged from nearby bushes and tip-toed up to him.

"Has he moved yet?" said Clare's voice.

"No," said Mot. "I'm frozen. I've been crouching here since midnight but he hasn't stirred."

Clare peered through the bushes at Gavin's house, its black outline clear against the night sky. Gavin's window in the tower remained blank.

"Do you think he went out of one of the doors?" asked Clare.

"No," said Mot. "I checked. They're all locked at night. It's the window or nothing. I'll go home now, Clare. I'll send Michael at 5 a.m. Let's check our watches."

They solemnly checked the time.

"I brought a flask, Clare," said Mot, "and some sandwiches. There's plenty left."

"Great stuff," said Clare. "Give me them and I'll tuck them in at the bottom of this tree."

She crawled into a little "hide" of branches that the Clan had prepared earlier. "So long, Mot," she said, easing herself into a comfortable position.

"So long, Clare," said Mot and disappeared into the darkness.

Clare gazed again at Gavin's window. She had four hours until Michael arrived. The Clan had been watching Gavin's window since midnight.

They were leaving nothing to chance.

Clare put her hand to her mouth. A sharp whistle rang through the trees, now lit by the morning sun.

Over on her right, Mot crawled out from underneath some bushes and looked over. He saw Clare's arm waving and beckoning.

Mot put his fingers in his mouth. The same whistle — the alarm call of a blackbird — rang out. Michael heard the call when he was halfway up an ash tree. He quickly slid down.

The two boys ran to where Clare was signalling.

"I've found him," she hissed, waving at them to crouch down.

"Where?" asked Mot.

"Beside the rocks, at the beech grove," said Clare. "I saw him on the path a few minutes ago. Then he hurried into the trees. I lost him after that."

"We can easily see him there," said Michael in a disappointed tone. "The trees are wide apart. Where could he hide there?"

"I don't know," said Mot, "but let's go and find out."

"All right," said Clare, "but let's take it slowly. He may be cleverer than we think. It may be a trick to throw us off the scent."

She began to weave her way through the trees, moving quickly and silently. The two boys trotted behind her, the bows on their backs bobbing up and down as they ran.

They slowed down as the trees thinned out into large glades. Clare dodged behind some bushes. Again, the two boys fell in behind her like obedient dogs.

Ahead of them was a clump of large rocks, covered in moss. All around grew huge beech trees, their light green leaves making a roof which cut off most of the sunlight, letting patches of yellow fall on their light grey bark.

Clare shaded her eyes with her hand. "Do you see him?" she asked.

Three pairs of eyes swept the trees and rocks. Mot and Michael shook their heads.

"Let's crawl to the rocks and see if we can spot him from there," said Clare.

She began to move slowly forward until she reached the base of the rocks. Then she crawled round the side. Mot and Michael watched silently. Then Clare's hand appeared round the side of the rock and waved twice.

The boys crawled over the leaves and grass until they, too, reached the rocks. Clare was crouching in a little gap. There was just room for the three of them. The boys slid silently in beside her.

"Any luck?" whispered Michael.

"Yes," said Clare. "But keep quiet. I want to see what he's up to. Besides we don't want to catch him now. Let's make a proper job of it and grab him when he's asleep in his hut."

"But we don't know where he'll sleep," said Mot.

"Yes, we do," said Clare. "What do you think he's doing here? He's building a hut. Take a look for yourself."

Mot peered over the edge of the rock. Down below, in a clearing in the trees, Gavin was piling branches together.

"What kind of hut is he making?" asked Michael.

"I don't know," said Clare in a bored tone. "He's picked an easy place to be found. The smoke of his fire would be seen for miles."

Michael took another look. "He's making a circle on the ground," he said.

Clare and Mot also peered over. Gavin was marking out a circle on the grass. The Clan watched silently as he took the branches and began sticking their thick ends into the earth, bringing the thin ends together in the centre.

"Will we grab him?" asked Mot.

"Och, no," said Clare. "It's too easy. Let's get him when he's asleep. Besides, if we dashed down now he might get away. It's a shame. Let's go back to the cave. One of us should stay here and keep an eye on him. It's your turn, Michael."

"All right," said the obliging Michael. "But how long do I have to stay?"

"Until he's made a proper hut," said Clare. "Then we'll know that he is not kidding us but will sleep there tonight."

"Come up to the cave when you can," said Mot.

"All right," said Michael. "If I'm late, I'll go straight back to the farm."

Clare and Mot crept round the boulder and out of sight. Michael made himself comfortable. If he leaned back he could just see Gavin through a notch in the rocks.

Down below Gavin was hard at work.

"I've got to make it look good," he thought. "They're bound to have followed me. So I'll make a really good job of it."

He made certain all his branches were pushed into the earth. Gathering together all the loose twiggy ends, he took a piece of string from his pocket. He tied the ends together.

Standing back, he surveyed the framework of his hut. "It's a bit like the African kraals I've seen on television," he thought. "Now I need lots of ferns and leafy branches." He pulled out his knife and began to cut huge armfuls of ferns and grass, plus all the small, leafy branches he could reach.

"Now for the roof," he thought. "It must look as if I am going to stay in it tonight." He began to weave the ferns in and out of the framework, plugging all the gaps with bunches of undergrowth and moss. His hut began to look like a small grass haystack.

Gavin stood back and looked at his handiwork. It

looked fine, a robust little shelter standing among the trees. He almost felt as if he did want to sleep in it.

He pondered for a moment, sitting down with his back against a tree. He tried to think like a Clansman.

"I've built my hut, it's quite well hidden. What else would I be expected to do?" He looked at the hut. It was rather easily seen. "I know. I'll camouflage it."

Gavin began to rake around the dead undergrowth of the glade. He hauled together piles of dead branches, and some of the remnants of the ones he had cut. He piled them together artistically near the hut, partially hiding it from view.

Then he walked through the trees and strolled casually past the hut. "Not bad at all," he thought. "I almost didn't notice it. I've built it and I've camouflaged it. Now I'll just make sure I could sleep in it."

He went to the small entrance he had made and crawled inside. It was quite dark. He had made the hut big enough to lie down. He stretched out for a moment on the ferns he had spread over the floor.

He looked up through the roof, squinting against the flashes of sunlight which had crept through the cracks. He sighed with contentment. It was a fine hut. Perhaps he might beat the Clan after all.

Above him, in the rocks, Michael continued his vigil.

He had carefully watched Gavin build his hut and try it out. He remained very still as Gavin shouldered his rucksack and set off through the trees for home.

Michael looked at his watch. It was time he went back to the farm.

Later that night, the Clan would return — to pounce on the sleeping Gavin as he lay in his hut.

"Poor chap," thought Michael. "All that work for nothing."

"Spread out in a circle," said Clare, a dark shadow

among the trees.

Mot and Michael crouched beside her. All three had blackened their faces and knees with soot so they would not be easily seen in the darkness.

"What will we do?" asked Mot.

Clare looked at her watch. "It's one a.m.," she said. "He's bound to be asleep by this time. But let's make sure he doesn't get away. We'll surround the hut, then creep up on him."

"What happens then?" asked Michael. "Will we burst in on him?"

Clare reflected for a moment. "No. That wouldn't be fair. I'll tap him on the shoulder and when he wakes, I'll say: 'Gavin, you are our prisoner. The Clan have won the contest'."

Michael and Mot looked suitably impressed. It sounded dramatic.

The three Clansmen peered over the rocks at the edge of the beech grove. Down below, a dark shadow in the moonlight, Gavin's hut stood among the trees.

Clare stood up. "I'll go round the back. Mot, take the left hand side. Michael, you come through these bushes over there."

"What if he makes a dash for it?" asked Michael.

"Chase him," said Clare. "If we get separated, we'll meet again at the farm. If we catch him, tap him on the arm and say he is a prisoner. Right, let's go."

Clare got down on all fours and wriggled through a gap in the rocks. Michael and Mot did the same, and crawled away into the darkness. There was no sound except the sighing of the night wind in the branches.

The three black shadows neared Gavin's hut. Clare raised a silent hand and the two boys rose to their feet.

They stood beside the entrance. Clare peered through the door. Lying inside was a long, black, sleeping body.

"He's there," she whispered. "Here goes." She tapped the figure on the shoulder. Nothing happened. She tapped again. Gavin seemed very stiff.

"What's wrong?" said Michael, puzzled by the silence. Mot prodded the figure with his bow through the hut entrance.

Clare felt in her anorak pocket and took out a torch. The beam of light cut through the darkness, and landed on an old coat.

"It's a dummy," gasped Clare, pulling the coat aside. Underneath was a pile of old clothes, laid out to look like a sleeping body. Beside the body was a heap of old cooking utensils.

Clare stamped her foot. "He's been cleverer than we thought," she said. "It's all been a trick. Where on earth can he be?"

"There's something else," said Michael, pointing at a white object on the hut floor.

"It's an envelope," said Mot picking it up. Clare tore it open.

She handed the torch to Michael. "Shine it here," she snapped. Inside the envelope was a plain white card. On it, in black letters, were the words: "Fooled You".

14   The Watcher Again

Gavin was involved in a family conference. He was eating his lunch.

Aunt Elspeth sat beside him. Uncle Fergus — bearded and silent — sat across from him. Occasionally, he gave Gavin a friendly smile.

"What are your plans for this afternoon and tomorrow, Gavin?" he asked.

"Oh, I'll just mooch around," said Gavin casually, although his heart was thumping with the thought of the Clan hunt.

"I'll be going into Stirling tomorrow and staying the night with a friend," said Aunt Elspeth. "But Betty will give you your meals and Uncle Fergus has agreed to tear himself away from his work to say hello to you now and again."

She smiled at Uncle Fergus, who grinned back.

"Just hammer on the library door if you want anything or feel like a chat," said Uncle Fergus. "Otherwise, just come and go as you please. I'll see you safely in bed at night though."

"All right," said Gavin. "You needn't worry, Aunt Elspeth. I'll be fine on my own. I've one or two things to do today and tomorrow anyway."

Aunt Elspeth, who had guessed he was up to some game with Clare and the others, nodded.

"I know you'll be sensible and not do anything silly. Now we'll let Uncle Fergus get back to his work. I'll be glad when it is finished. Having such a lot of silver in the house makes me nervous."

"Och, it's well looked after," rumbled Uncle Fergus, getting up.

"Enjoy yourself, Gavin, and — don't forget — if you

want anything bang on the door. Bang hard, because once I get involved in my writing I don't hear anything."

"You can say that again," said Aunt Elspeth. "The number of meals you've missed!"

Chuckling, Gavin left the table and hurried to his room. He wanted to think over his plan of campaign.

He'd spent that morning building his decoy hut in the woods. Now he wanted to get ready for his afternoon and night in the hidden castle.

He made up his mind. He would take his gear to the castle that afternoon and dump it there. He would return to the house, say goodnight to Uncle Fergus and go to his room.

Once it was dark, he would slip out of the house and go back to the castle and stay there until morning. He began to get his gear together.

Gavin was blissfully happy. He had scored off the Clan. They had been so busy watching his decoy hut that he had had no difficulty in throwing them off his tracks.

Elated, he had hurried through the woods to the hidden castle. There, he had laid out his groundsheet and sleeping bag, eaten a few sandwiches, and fallen asleep watching the stars through the dark waving branches of the trees.

He had woken up once or twice in the night, but on the whole he had slept quite well.

He awoke in the early hours of the morning. The sun shone through the trees. All around birds were in full song. There was a fresh smell of earth and leaves wet with dew.

Gavin stretched luxuriously, then got out of his sleeping bag. He had slept with most of his clothes on.

Walking to the little stream which trickled down the rocks, he splashed his face and hands with water and dried himself on his handkerchief. Now for breakfast. He pulled out Mot's notes and samples and examined them closely.

Kindling wood was needed — that meant soft woods like birch, ash or fir. Then harder wood to keep the fire going — oak, or indeed anything once there was a blaze.

He examined the trees. The birch was easy — slim silver trunk, feathery, light green leaves. There were several near by. Gavin examined their branches, breaking off all the dead wood he could see.

The yew trees at the entrance of the castle also had plenty of dead wood on lower branches. Soon he had a fine pile. He took it back to his fireplace and dropped it on the ground. Then he raked around until he found larger, chunkier pieces and piled them up as well.

Gavin hummed happily to himself. He was enjoying this feeling of being alone, of being in the woods and yet being able to look after himself. With Mot's notes to help him, he had not found it too difficult finding suitable wood.

He examined the cliff-fireplace. At its foot was a small recess at the bottom of the rock. It was open for about three or four feet then it disappeared inside the rock, just like a real chimney.

Gavin consulted his notes again. Ah, now he remembered. He searched round until he found a firm piece of wood, shaped like a catapult in the form of a "Y". With his knife he sharpened it to a point and then pushed it into the earth.

Then he broke off the smallest twigs, little thicker than a matchstick and piled them up against the crossed stick so that they resembled a little tepee with a gap at one side.

He sat back on his heels and looked at it. What next? He moved some of the stones in the fireplace closer to the wood. They were large and flat-topped and would hold his dixie firmly over the flames.

Then he took out his matches. Only two were

permitted, the Clan said. He struck one. It spluttered and went out before he could apply it to the small sticks and dead leaves.

He struck another. The wood curled and blackened. A thin wisp of smoke went up. Gavin watched anxiously. Then more flames appeared. In a minute, his pile of kindling was burning steadily.

Carefully, Gavin laid on larger pieces and, when they were alight, he piled on some large, chunky logs. They would burn more slowly and would provide a steady flame. They would also do as a base for his dixie.

There was very little smoke, showing the wood was dry and dead. Mot had told him that wet wood or green wood gave off lots of smoke, so Gavin had been very careful to look for dry spots.

He filled his dixie with water and put it on the fire, balancing it carefully on the stones.

Soon the water sent up hordes of tiny bubbles, then the whole surface gurgled and boiled. Gavin dropped in three handfuls of porridge oats, making sure he stirred steadily all the time to avoid lumps. He sprinkled in a little salt. After a few minutes, the porridge was ready, hot and thick.

Gavin lifted the dixie off the fire with the bulldog grip, the metal claws gripping the edge tightly. He sprinkled on a little sugar, added some milk from a carton he had put in his rucksack and ate steadily.

He looked at his watch. The hands pointed to 5 a.m. He had plenty of time before hurrying back to the house for lunch. He had left a note saying he was "skipping" breakfast as he was out for a walk.

Aunt Elspeth and Uncle Fergus did not know he had been out of the house all night, so he would have to slip in quietly. Then he had to evade the Clan all day, until midnight that night. The rules of the hunt were that he had to cook one meal. So far, he was halfway through that without any mishap.

After eating his porridge, Gavin ate the rest of his

soggy sandwiches. He reflected on his plans. He decided to hang around the castle until late morning, then to return to the castle later and lie up there until dark.

He decided to have some tea. He scraped all the porridge dregs out of the dixie and put them into a small hole he had dug in the leafy soil near the entrance to the castle. Then he covered them over. The Clan never left litter. Besides, litter might be a clue to where he had been.

He filled the dixie with water again. When the water boiled it removed the remainder of the porridge which swirled around in the water. Gavin emptied the water out. The dixie was clean again, but he gave it a wipe with some grass just to make sure.

Then he refilled it and piled more wood on the fire. Soon the flames were roaring up the chimney again. Gavin put the dixie back on again.

He took the small tea-leaves holder from his rucksack, and hooked it on to the side of the dixie. Soon the water boiled and turned brown. Gavin lifted it off the fire again and poured it into his aluminium cup. He added sugar and milk and drank slowly. It was good, hot and sweet.

He leaned against the rock enjoying the feeling of well-being, the sun on his face and the silence of the woods all around. The birds had stopped their morning chorus as the sun had risen higher in the sky, and were on the hunt for food.

Robins, chaffinches and thrushes perched on the trees around the castle, hoping for some scraps. Remembering the story of the babes in the wood and how their bread trail was eaten up, Gavin threw some crumbs to the side and sat still. Soon the small woodland birds were pecking busily.

After a time Gavin decided to go home. He packed up his gear, poured the dregs of the tea on the fire until the last ember had been quenched, and then scattered the black sticks among the trees.

He covered the black fireplace with dead leaves and earth. Soon the castle looked as if no one had visited it for years.

Gavin climbed to the top of the tower and looked all around. The woods seemed silent. Quietly, he picked his way down to the bottom of the crags.

Then walking quietly he moved through the trees in the direction of the house. Soon he saw its red roof and his bedroom turret.

But just before he stepped out of the bushes on to the path he saw something which made him stand very still.

Lying on the ground near the top of a small rise was a man.

15 The Final Round

Gavin ducked down behind the bushes. What was the man up to?

He remembered what Mot had said about stalking: "Keep very still, remember your face shows like a white blob over a long distance. If you have to move . . . do so very slowly and steadily. Freeze at the slightest hint of being seen."

Slowly, Gavin raised his head until he could see through the leaves.

The man was examining the house through binoculars. Then he laid them down and took out a notebook. He wrote in it for some minutes, then picked up his binoculars again.

Gavin watched him closely. He decided to get closer. There was something sinister about this hidden watcher.

Slowly Gavin lay down on the ground and began a steady crawl through the trees towards the man. He remembered his lesson with Mot and examined the ground ahead for dry leaves and twigs before he made his next move.

He moved very slowly, stopping to raise his head carefully and see if the man was still there. Once he stopped and froze as the man stirred and sat up. But after glancing all round him the man lay down again.

By this time Gavin could see he was wearing a dark blue suit and black shoes. He could not see his face for the man was looking away from him, towards the house.

Gavin thought hard. What was he looking at? Perhaps if he, Gavin, could crawl round behind him he might see what the man was examining so closely.

He set out again. Soon he was directly behind him. Gavin crawled behind the wide trunk of a beech tree.

Then he stood up, taking care to keep the trunk between himself and the man.

He peeped round the corner. The man was just a few yards ahead. Gavin looked beyond him. Through a gap in the trees he could see the front door of Aunt Elspeth's house. He could also see the wide window of Uncle Fergus's study. Indeed, he could see Uncle Fergus working at his desk.

As he watched, the front door opened and Aunt Elspeth came down the steps. She opened the door of her car, and drove off down the drive.

As she did so, the man got up. He put the notebook and binoculars in the pocket of his jacket. Then he walked straight towards the tree where Gavin was hiding.

Gavin again tried to remember Mot's advice. "Keep very still," he had said, "and the chances are you will not be seen." So Gavin crouched at the foot of the tree and hardly dared breathe.

The footsteps crunched nearer and nearer. Out of the corner of his eye, Gavin could see the shape of the man looming nearer. Quite distinctly, he saw a black shoe and trousered leg swing past him, only a few feet away ... and the man was soon lost among the trees.

Gavin let his breath out with a gasp. Then he straightened up slowly. It had been a close shave. The man had been near enough to touch. What on earth had he been up to?

Gavin thought about the mystery as he hurried home, only stopping at each bend in the path to examine the way ahead in case the Clan were planning to ambush him.

Anyway, he decided, he would tell Uncle Fergus when he got home that he had seen a strange man examining the house through binoculars.

Meantime, the Clan were in council. Clare sat on a log, surrounded by Mot and Michael.

"We've got to catch him," she said. "We can't have someone from England beating us in our own woods. Let's have some ideas. Where can he be?"

Mot chimed in: "He clearly had this well planned. He spent a lot of time building a dummy hut to throw us off the scent. That would mean he didn't have time to build another hut."

"Good man," said Clare. "That's the stuff we want."

"I agree," said Michael. "He couldn't build two huts. He took a lot of trouble to build a decent hut. After all, it was good enough to sleep in and to fool us."

"That's right," said Clare. "There's only one other solution. He must be either in a cave or a hut of some kind, a hut already built that is."

"He's not in a cave," said Michael. "We know all the caves in the area. And he would know that we know."

"And there are no huts," said Mot. Silence fell while the three thought hard.

Then Clare gasped. "I've got it," she said. "Why didn't I think of it before. He's a stranger here. He either built a hut himself — in which case we would have found out — or he asked someone to think of a hiding place for him."

"His aunt!" said Mot.

"That's it," said Michael.

"Right," said Clare. "His aunt must have told him of somewhere and that means an area near their house. After all, we don't go into that section of the woods very often. There could be places we haven't seen."

She looked up at the sun, glinting through the leaves.

"It's just about breakfast time," she said. "Let's hurry home, get something to eat, then we'll tackle the woods near the house. We've still got until tonight to catch him."

"He slept out last night though," said Mot. "It's not going to be so easy."

"I know," said Michael. "But he's not allowed to

hang around the house all day. He must stay in the woods or on the hills until midnight tonight. Do you think he just spent the night sleeping on the ground, say at the bottom of a tree or in some bushes or somewhere like that?''

"No, I don't think so," said Mot. "He's got a proper hideout somewhere all right. The point is, where? Even if he isn't in it now, he may well be in that area. We might get some clues as to where he is."

"Yes, that's sensible," said Clare. "We've got to find him today. It's going to be harder than yesterday. He won the first round by letting us think he was in that hut. Now, instead of pinning him down in one spot he can be anywhere in the whole area."

Mot chimed in again: "And he needn't return to his aunt's house at all all day if he's got enough food."

"I think we should take the area near his aunt's house and search it thoroughly," said Michael.

Clare thought hard for a moment. "Okay," she said. "Here's the plan. We all go back for breakfast, then we set out again for the woods near Gavin's house. We spend the rest of the day searching for him there."

"I suggest we take a section each and report to one another twice," she continued. "Once at Owl's Tree — you all know the spot — at teatime, and the second at ten o'clock at the same place. If we haven't found him by then, we have no choice but to go up to the cave and wait for Gavin. That will be the end of the game, and Gavin will have won," she added gloomily.

Then she smiled. "But we've got lots of time until then. We'll catch him. Is that settled?" Michael and Mot nodded.

"Now to details," said Clare. "We'll need enough food each to last us until night-time."

"Will we wear full uniform?" asked Michael.

"Oh yes," said Clare. "This is the final round. We must do things properly — anoraks, balmorals, tartan sashes and bows. We *must* catch him. Now, let's go home and eat and get started."

The three got to their feet and trotted briskly off though the trees.

This time, they meant business.

16 Signs of Alarm

Gavin raced into the house, his breath coming in gasps. He dumped his rucksack on the doorstep and headed for the kitchen door. He skidded on the rug at the entrance to the kitchen, and caught hold of the side of the door to keep his balance.

A muffled exclamation came from a cupboard. Betty, the maid, came out with a startled look on her face.

"My goodness me!" she said. "Whatever is the matter?"

"Where's Uncle Fergus?" said Gavin.

"He's just gone out for a walk," said Betty. "Why?"

"Why?" echoed Gavin. "There's a man watching the house through binoculars, that's why! Where did Uncle Fergus go? When will he be back? Quick, it's important."

He hopped excitedly from one foot to the other.

"Now just calm yourself," said Betty. "Your uncle has only gone for a walk. He'll be back soon. He's been in his study for days. He needed some air, he said. What's all this about a man?"

Gavin began to tell her, the words pouring out of him at first, then coming more slowly as he went on. As he told her what he had seen, it didn't sound quite so alarming as he had thought at first.

Betty listened intently and patiently as he told her about seeing the man lying behind a tree watching the house through binoculars, of how he had hidden when the man left after Aunt Elspeth had driven off in her car.

"I don't know what he was up to," he finished lamely. "But people don't hide behind trees for nothing. There's a lot of silver in the house. For all we know he might have been after that. Do you think we should phone the police?''

Betty thought for a moment, her brow frowning. Gavin began to dance with impatience.

''I think *someone* should be told,'' he said. ''Have you any idea where Uncle Fergus has gone? Perhaps I could go and find him.''

''You could try,'' said Betty doubtfully. ''But I don't know which way he went. I'm a bit worried myself. I've never liked having all that silver in the house. I know it's in a safe, but this is quite a lonely house.''

Then she brightened up. ''Perhaps he's just a poacher,'' she said. ''No one knows there is silver here. Only your uncle and aunt and yourself. I know, because I have to clean the house and I was told about it. But no one else knows.''

''I'm sure your uncle will be back any minute,'' continued Betty. ''He'll know what to do.'' She smiled at Gavin. ''Besides, you and I are in the house. No one is going to come in now. It'll be hours before it is dark, and your uncle will be back by then.''

Gavin thought hard. Perhaps he *was* letting his imagination run away with him. Perhaps being hunted by the Clan had affected him.

Thinking of the Clan reminded him that he was not supposed to stay in the house. Then an idea struck him.

''I've got an idea,'' he said to Betty who still had a worried look on her face. ''I'll phone Aunt Elspeth, and tell her about it. She'll know all about poachers and tramps and can tell us what to do. Where's the phone book?''

Betty brightened up. ''That's a good idea,'' she said. She found the directory and thumbed through the pages.

''Here it is,'' she said, her finger on a number. ''Mrs Ross, that's your aunt's friend — Stirling 61316. Will you speak to her or will I?''

''It would be better if you spoke, Betty,'' said Gavin. ''She'll perhaps get very worried if I phone.''

Betty picked up the receiver and dialled the number. Gavin could hear the distant ringing of the phone, but no one answered.

"I'll try again," said Betty. She re-dialled. Again the faint sound of the ringing, brrr-brrr brrr-brrr, could be heard.

Gavin felt the silence was becoming a little sinister. "Do you think we should lock the doors and barricade the house?" he said with a half-smile.

Betty put down the receiver. "Get away with you," she said. "We're letting our imaginations run away with us. Just because of an old poacher in the woods! Why, he might have been a bird watcher like yourself."

"That's true," said Gavin. He might have been a bird watcher. That would explain the binoculars.

Worry nagged at his mind. Bird watchers didn't normally watch houses through binoculars. It was odd the phone ringing out like that. Aunt Elspeth had said she would be at her friend's house.

"How far is it from here to the nearest house?" he asked Betty.

"To the nearest house?" said Betty in surprise. "Why it's all of two miles. You're not thinking of walking there are you? Your uncle will be back soon, I'm sure."

"I'll tell you what," she went on, "I'll just pop along to the study and make sure everything is in the safe. There's nothing else in the house worth stealing," she added with a grin.

Gavin followed her along the passage and up the stairs to the study. Betty opened the door.

The library table was strewn with paper and notebooks. Old crates stood on the floor. Piles of books were strewn around. Everything was in confusion.

But there was no silver. And the door of the safe was tightly shut.

"He's an awfully untidy worker," said Betty. "But that's a relief. All the silver is in the safe. Are you happy now?" she asked Gavin.

Gavin's fears vanished. "Yes, that's fine, Betty," he said. "I'm sorry to get you alarmed."

"Oh, don't bother about that," said Betty. "There's some odd characters in the world. You were quite right to be careful. What are you going to do until evening?"

"I'm going for a stroll in the woods," said Gavin. "I'll stay near the house, so if Uncle Fergus comes back I can talk to him."

"That's the best plan," said Betty. "If I see him first, I'll tell him what you saw. I'll put the snib on the front and back doors so if anyone wants in, they'll have to ring the bell or knock on the door — even if it is you or your uncle!"

"Right," said Gavin. "If it is me, I'll give three rings so you know it's me."

He went up to his room and left all the stuff he had brought home from the castle. He put an apple and orange and two bars of chocolate in his pocket and sauntered out again.

He peered carefully round the door, scanning the edge of the wood. There was no sign of either the Clan or the mysterious stranger. It was time to get on with the Clan contest.

Gavin decided he would prowl around the woods near the house, and perhaps find somewhere handy to hole up if the Clan should be near.

He examined the trees again. There was no sign of any movement. He darted quickly across the lawn and vanished in the trees.

17 The Three Prisoners

Gavin woke up with a start. Water dripped on his face. He felt cold and stiff.

"Gosh!" he thought, "I must have fallen asleep. I must have been here for hours."

He hurriedly looked around, and then squinted up at the darkening sky. Raindrops plopped slowly on to his anorak and then increased until it began to rain steadily. He had been lying in a little clearing at the edge of the woods.

"Why, it's evening!" he said in surprise. "I must have been more tired than I thought. I expect it's because I was too excited to sleep properly when I was in the castle last night."

He chuckled to himself. His luck was certainly in. Any of the Clan could have bumped right into him, lying there asleep like that.

He looked back towards the house, now a dark shadow against the overcast sky. There was something odd about it, he thought. There wasn't a light on. Not one. Normally, a light would twinkle from the kitchen or Uncle Fergus's study. But now all was dark.

"How odd," thought Gavin. "Perhaps they've had a power cut."

He walked slowly towards the house. Then he remembered. Aunt Elspeth had left to go into town. That would explain her absence. Uncle Fergus might still be out for his walk. He quickened his steps and pushed open the front door.

The hall was in darkness. He found the light switch and pressed it. Nothing happened. He felt his way along the corridor to the kitchen door and tried to push it open. It was shut tight. Gavin gave it a hard push. It seemed locked.

How very strange. "Betty! Betty!" he called out, his voice echoing in the dark house.

Then through the shut kitchen door he thought he heard a slight sound, like a whimper. Gavin began to get frightened. He felt his way along the corridor again towards Uncle Fergus's room. He called out: "Uncle! Uncle Fergus-s-s-s!"

Still there was not a sound, except the scrape of Gavin's boots as he felt his way along the wall.

Then a hand fastened itself over his mouth, and another grabbed him by the waist and threw him to the floor, pinning him to the ground.

Gavin nearly fainted. The hot hand slapped across his mouth made his heart leap into his throat and for a moment he thought he was going to die of fright.

Clearly, no ghost had grabbed him. It was a man. He could feel his clothes with his hand and his knee on his legs where he was pinned to the floor.

Then he had an idea. He bit the hand across his mouth with all his might. A man's voice swore, and for a moment Gavin was free.

He shouted: "Help! Help!" at the top of his voice, twisted on the floor and got loose. He kicked out and the hard toe of his climbing boots encountered human flesh. There was another outburst of swearing.

"Uncle Fergus! Uncle Fergus!" bellowed Gavin again, as he desperately tried to run for the door.

"It's a kid," said a voice.

"Get him. Get him, before he gets out, Willie. Get to the door, you fool."

Gavin crouched low in the darkened hall. His eyes were becoming used to the dark and he thought he saw the shadows of the two men.

"Do you see him?" said a voice in a whisper.

"Nah. Work towards the door," said the second voice. "He can't get out of this room. Keep an eye on the stairs."

Gavin crouched still, remembering Mot's advice about stillness being the best help to being unseen. The dark figures moved slowly towards him.

"Hi! Hi! Kid," said a voice. Gavin stayed silent and motionless.

"We won't hurt you. You're only making it worse for yourself. Give yourself up, and I promise you won't get hurt." Still Gavin stayed quiet.

"Okay, kid," said the voice. "Play it the hard way, if you like. Move up here wi' me, Pete. He's at the top end somewhere."

Gavin waited for a moment, and thought desperately. They must be burglars. After the silver. Perhaps Betty was tied up in the kitchen. Uncle Fergus must be out of the house or their prisoner or worse. He gulped. He must get out of the house and raise the alarm.

Summoning up his courage, he made a dash for what was the front door and crashed head over heels over a large object. He had fallen over the hall chair. He lay dazed for a moment. Before he could move, huge hands grabbed him again. This time there was no escape.

"I've got him," said a voice triumphantly.

"Good man, Pete," said the other. "Bring him upstairs. Keep him quiet. There's been enough noise in here already."

The hands lifted Gavin, as a terrier lifts a rat, by the scruff of the neck and shook him.

"Listen, you," said the voice of the one called Pete. "If you promise to keep quiet, I'll let your mouth go. But it you struggle or shout out again, then I'll punch you silly and gag you." He shook Gavin again until his head swam.

"Nod your head, if you agree," he said. Hurriedly, Gavin nodded. The hand released his mouth. He sucked in breath hurriedly.

"Come with us," said the voice. They tugged Gavin through the dark hall and up the stairs to the first floor. They seemed to be heading for Uncle Fergus's room.

Once or twice one of the men stumbled and swore. They didn't seem to be familiar with the house.

"Where is it, Pete?" said one voice.

"This is it. It's the one at the end. I can see Cobra's light."

Gavin peered ahead as he was manhandled along the passage. Sure enough, there was a faint glimmer of light from under Uncle Fergus's door. One of the men rapped on the door.

"It's us, Cobra. Open the door. We've got a kid. It's the one who lives in the house."

"Okay, I'm opening up," said a voice from inside the room.

The men bundled Gavin into the room and he stared around. Uncle Fergus was sitting bound and gagged in a chair.

"Uncle!" he cried, and started forward.

"Oh, no you don't!" said the man called Pete and grabbed him by the arms. Gavin wondered if he should kick out again, then decided against it.

He gave a quick glance around the room. The windows were closed and shuttered, and the room was lit by a small hand lamp set on Uncle Fergus's desk. Uncle Fergus sat still, but one of his eyelids winked twice at Gavin as if to reassure him.

Two men stood by the desk. They were wearing masks over the lower parts of their faces, with a hole cut for the mouth.

One was tall and thin, with a narrow face rather like a snake. Gavin could see why the others called him Cobra. Even with a mask he looked snake-like. The other man was smaller. So far he had not spoken.

"What's your name?" asked Cobra.

"Gavin," said Gavin.

Cobra was silent for a moment. Then he turned to the other two.

"Give you a bit of trouble, did he?" The two men shuffled sheepishly. "Did he make any noise," Cobra asked.

"Nah. We grabbed him in the hall. He tried to bolt out of the door," said Pete.

Gavin studied the men. He would try and remember them all later.

All four looked about twenty-five, he thought, but two might be older. They wore old clothes, but the small man beside Uncle Fergus's chair wore overalls. They looked dirty and down at heel, as if they had lived rough. They also looked rather frightening with their masks and truculent air.

Cobra spoke again: "Sit in that chair, kid, and keep your mouth shut. Pete, stand behind him. If he makes a sound, hit him hard."

Gavin sat down, very quietly, on the nearest chair. Pete stood beside him.

"Willie!" said Cobra. "Check the windows. Make sure no light will show outside."

Willie examined the windows and heavy curtains. "All secure, boss," he said.

"Right," said Cobra. "Turn up the lamp a little."

Willie moved to the table and gave a handle on the lamp a few twists. The room lightened.

All this time Uncle Fergus had sat quite still, but his eyes looked anxious except when they caught Gavin's. Then he tried to wink reassuringly.

Cobra was clearly the boss, Gavin thought. He gave all the orders.

Cobra spoke again. "Alex, go down to the kitchen. Check that the maid is still tied up. Check the front door and all downstairs windows. Lock the lot. Don't lock the back door, but fasten it tightly from the inside."

"Okay, Cobra," said the man called Alex.

"One other thing," said Cobra. "Stay at the front windows. Anywhere you like, but don't be seen. If there's the slightest sign of any danger, warn us in here."

Alex nodded. Cobra spoke again.

"Have a quick squint outside before you lock up. See if our light shows outside. It shouldn't with both shutters and curtains up, but we must be certain. Come back and tell me before you settle down at the front."

Alex nodded to all these instructions and left.

Pete continued to stand guard beside Gavin, and Willie stood beside Uncle Fergus. Cobra continued to question Gavin.

"Are you the only person in the house?" Gavin nodded.

Cobra turned to Uncle Fergus. "I want some answers from you. If I think you're lying, the kid gets it. Do you understand?"

Uncle Fergus nodded slowly.

"And another thing," said Cobra. "One of us will be standing beside the boy all the time. Make any trouble and we clobber him."

He produced a knife from his pocket, pressed a small switch and a long blade flicked out. Gavin gasped.

Cobra smiled slowly. It was not a pleasant smile.

"You get the idea, kid?" he said. "You too, pal?" ... to Uncle Fergus.

Uncle Fergus nodded.

"Okay," said Cobra. "Take his gag off. But make sure he's still tied up."

Willie checked the ropes which held Uncle Fergus tightly to the chair.

"All right, Cobra. He'll no' move from that."

"Right, then," said Cobra. "Let's get down to business. We're wasting time."

He pulled a chair forward, and sat down. There was a moment's silence while he pulled a cigarette from his pocket and lit it. Before he could speak, there came a tap at the door.

"It's me, lads," said Alex's voice. Willie opened the door. Alex stuck his head round.

"It's all right, boss," he said. "The lassie in the kitchen is still tied up and not uttering a sound. I waved a kitchen knife in front of her just to show who's boss. I think she fainted. Anyhow, she can't move and can't speak.''

He chuckled. ''Your light can't be seen from the outside. Not a chink,'' he told Cobra.

''Thanks,'' said Cobra. ''Get back to the front of the house. Keep watch! I'll send Willie along when we're ready to blow.'' Alex disappeared out of the door.

Cobra turned to the others. ''Take his gag off,'' he told Pete.

Pete bent over Uncle Fergus and removed the scarf which had been used as a gag. Uncle Fergus moved his lips around, and swallowed once or twice, as he tried to get rid of the feel of the gag.

''Are you and the kid the only people in the house, other than the maid?'' he asked Uncle Fergus.

''Yes,'' said Uncle Fergus, and coughed as his dry throat made him choke a little.

He coughed again, then said: ''Look here, I don't know what you want but there's no money in this house. You'll never get away with breaking in here. There's a party of people due here this evening, so you'd better clear out quickly while you've still got the chance.''

Cobra smiled his unpleasant smile.

''Who are you trying to kid, cock?'' he said. ''We've been watching this house for weeks. There's only yourself and your wife and the maid. The maid's tied up, and your wife stays in Stirling every Friday night. We haven't spent hours watching you for nothing. We've seen this kid staying here. Who is he, anyway?''

''He's a nephew. He's on holiday with us,'' said Uncle Fergus. ''Leave him out of it. Why not let him go?''

''He stays here,'' said Cobra. ''And don't give me all that codswallop about no money in the house. You've got silver here. You've had it here for weeks. I know most of it is here at the moment, because we've watched your journeys into town.''

"Some of that stuff is priceless," he went on. "It's in this house somewhere and I'm going to find out where. And you're going to tell us."

He moved over to Uncle Fergus's chair and stood in front of him.

18 Raiders at Work

Uncle Fergus thought for a moment and then said quietly: "Search the house, if you like. I'll tell you nothing."

Cobra pulled a knife out of his pocket and held it against Uncle Fergus's throat.

"Don't waste our time, wise man. I *know* the stuff is in the house. It's probably in that safe." He pointed to the green-painted safe which stood in a corner of the room.

"But I'm not wasting time," he went on. "If you don't tell us, then the kid gets hurt. "Hold him, Willie!" he snapped.

Willie grabbed Gavin by the shoulders and held him on to the chair. Cobra moved menacingly over to Gavin.

"You've got four seconds," he told Uncle Fergus. "You either tell us where the silver is, or I ask Willie to give the kid a prod with his knife."

"Then you'll get another four seconds," said Cobra, "and if you aren't co-operating by then the boy will get some more. Now, where's the silver? One ... two ... three ..."

Uncle Fergus spoke hurriedly. "Leave the boy alone. I'll tell you where it is. It's in the safe. But it's got a time lock." He smiled triumphantly. "It won't open until tomorrow morning, and by that time it will be daylight and people will be about."

"It's too heavy for you to move," went on Uncle Fergus. "So you're not so clever after all. A closed safe isn't much use to you. I suggest you get out of here quickly while you still have time. Go and look for yourself if you don't believe the safe has a time lock."

"Oh, I can see it's got a time lock all right," said

Cobra smoothly. "It could have thirty locks for all I care. All I wanted to know was what was inside. And now we know!"

He turned to Gavin. "Sit where you are, boy, and you'll not get hurt. Willie, get along to the front door and tell Alex to get back here. And tell him to fetch his stuff from the car."

Gavin pricked up his ears. So they had a car. That was useful information. He set himself to remember every scrap of information he could so that he could help the police later.

Willie opened the door and went out. Cobra sat on the edge of the table.

"I know you've got quite a lot of stuff in there," he said conversationally to Uncle Fergus. "We've seen the journeys you've made, and we've checked up on what you're doing. Some of that old Scots silver will fetch high prices abroad."

"Look!" said Uncle Fergus. "Why don't you let the boy go? He needn't be here at all. Let him go and he'll promise not to contact the police for two hours or whatever time you like. Won't you, Gavin?"

"Nothing doing!" said Cobra before Gavin could speak. "I give the orders. And I say we all stay here for the moment."

Just then the door opened and Alex came in.

"Bill at his post?" inquired Cobra. Alex nodded. "Okay," said Cobra. "Take a look at that safe in the corner."

Alex examined the safe carefully, running his hands over the sides and tapping on the door with his fingers, then listening with his ear to the door.

"Well?" said Cobra impatiently. "Any trouble? Can you do it?"

Alex nodded. He was apparently a man of few words.

"It's easy, boss. It's got a good time lock all right, but I can blow it."

"Great!" said Cobra. "How long will you need?"

Alex thought for a moment.

"Half an hour will do, but I'll need mattresses and other stuff to muffle the bang. The room will need to be cleared."

Cobra spoke again. "Pete, you scour the house. Tell Willie to stay at the front and keep watch. Tell him we're going to blow in half an hour, but he's not to leave until we're all ready to leave for good. Bring back mattresses, blankets, pillows, stuff like that. Got it?"

"Yes," said Pete shortly. "What about these two?" he said, pointing to Gavin and Uncle Fergus.

"Alex and I will stay here," said Cobra. "Get cracking!"

Cobra continued to sit on the table, his legs swinging. Uncle Fergus and Gavin sat silently, watching him.

Alex busied himself moving furniture away from the safe, until he had cleared a space around it. Occasionally, he grunted to himself.

The door opened, and Pete backed into the room dragging a mattress behind him.

"There's plenty of stuff," he said. "But the house is very dark. Can I have another torch?"

Cobra took one from his jacket pocket and handed it over. "Alex!" he said. "Go and give Pete a hand. We must hurry things up."

Alex and Pete went out and returned three times with piles of mattresses and blankets.

"That enough?" queried Cobra.

"Yes, that'll do," said Alex. "Now leave me to set it up. Half an hour should do. If I don't bust it open first time, I may have to have another go. That'll be tricky if the safe is slit. I don't want to damage the stuff inside."

"All right! All right!" said Cobra impatiently. "How long if you need two goes at it?"

"An hour to an hour and a half should do it."

Cobra grunted angrily. "It's taking longer every time I ask you!" he said.

"I know, Cobra, I know," said Alex. "But I've never seen this safe before. It's an old-fashioned type, and they can stand a lot of explosive."

"Well, get to work," Cobra said. "We'll all go down to the kitchen and get something to eat. But first, we'll lock up this pair in case we have to leave in a hurry."

He turned to Pete. "Put the man in the kitchen with the maid, and tie their chairs together. Put his gag back on."

He turned to Gavin. "Where's your room, kid?" he said.

"At the top of the stairs," said Gavin.

"Pete!" said Cobra. "After you've got Uncle here into the kitchen, take the boy to his room. Make sure he can't get out. Check the window. Tie him to his bed."

"Be sure and make a good job of it," snapped Cobra. "Make sure he can't break the glass of the window. Don't be too rough on him, he's been sensible so far."

Pete bent down to untie Uncle Fergus's legs, and then he and Alex marched him from the room.

Cobra stayed with Gavin.

"Now, look here, kid," said Cobra. "I don't want to hurt you, but we've got to lock you away for a bit ... just until we finish what we've got to do here. Sit down there and keep quiet until the boys come back."

Gavin subsided quietly on to one of the chairs. He made up his mind that his best plan was to say as little as possible, notice as much as he could, and try and make a break for it if an opportunity presented itself.

The door opened and Pete returned.

"Take the kid to his room," said Cobra. "Don't gag him if you're sure he can't be heard. Make sure he can't get out of the window. So long, kid."

He gave Gavin a clump on the back, and then Gavin found himself gripped firmly by Pete and marched out of the room.

"Where's your room?" said Pete gruffly.

106

"Top of the stairs," said Gavin. "I already told you."

"Lead on then, but don't try any tricks."

Still firmly gripped, Gavin climbed up the stairs. Occasionally, he stumbled. The stairs were only lit by Pete's hand-torch.

"This is it," said Gavin as he arrived at his door.

"Inside!" said Pete tersely.

Pete flashed his torch around the room. Then a voice spoke behind him. It was Cobra. He was taking no chances.

"Just thought I'd take a look myself," he said. "Pete, stay at the door while I have a look at the window. We've got some time to wait while Alex does his stuff with the safe."

Gavin stood still in the middle of his room. A dozen uncompleted plans raced through his head.

Cobra spoke again. "He can get out of this window, though it's a long way from the ground. Got a clasp knife?"

Pete felt in his pocket and handed one over. Cobra bent over the window catch, and then grunted hard with effort.

"That's it! I've bent the catch down. No one's opening that window. And he can't break the glass. We'll hear it from below. Tie him to his bed. Make sure he's comfortable, but can't reach either the door or the window, even if the window *is* fastened."

Pete took some rope from his pocket, passed some coils round Gavin's wrists and pulled them tight. Gavin winced as the ropes bit into his wrists.

"Sorry, kid," said Pete. "It's for your own good."

He made Gavin sit down on the bed, and then tied his legs together, finally tying a large loop round the legs of the bed. Gavin found he could move his body a little, but not very far. But he wasn't too uncomfortable, sitting up like that.

"Finished?" said Cobra.

107

"That's the lot," said Pete.

"Then get back down below and help Alex," said Cobra. "Take a look at the kitchen on your way down. I don't want any mistakes." Pete left.

"So long, kid," said Cobra. "Somebody will be here to let you out in the morning."

He closed the door and Gavin heard the key turn in the lock.

19   The Distress Signal

Gavin sat in the dark room. Outside the window the night sky was a dark blue. A few stars twinkled palely.

His heart raced and thumped. He realised with a start that he was really quite frightened. The men had treated him with a mixture of roughness and threats and, occasionally, kindness.

He wondered why they had put Uncle Fergus and himself in different rooms. Then he realised. If any one of them got free, they still had to get out of the locked room. One person would find it harder to break down a locked door alone.

He imagined that Betty would be in such a hysterical state that, even if she got free, she wouldn't be of much help.

He wondered what he should do. It would be no use shouting. No one could hear.

Perhaps he could get himself untied. Gavin found he could move his hands a fraction, but his wrists were very tightly bound together. He could move his legs just a little.

If only he could make some sort of signal. But who would see it? Then he remembered. The Clan were out that night. They might see it. But where would they be? Gavin thought frantically. "I wonder what the time is," he thought suddenly. After wriggling around he managed to get a look at his watch. It was eleven o'clock. In an hour his game with the Clan ended.

"At least I won," he thought wryly. "I'm a Clan member."

He wondered for a moment if Clare would accept his membership when he had spent some of the game indoors. He reckoned that the fact of the burglars making him stay would count in his favour.

He knew the Clan would be going to the cave. Perhaps he could signal there? They might see the signals going up the hill. Once they were in the cave it would take too long before they could get back down.

How long did he have?

Gavin tried to remember every scrap of conversation that had taken place in his uncle's study.

The men were trying to blow up the safe. If the explosives worked, then about half an hour would be the time.

If the men had to make a second attempt, about an hour, perhaps longer. There was still time to do something.

He just *had* to find a way to signal.

Frantically, he began to push and wriggle with his feet to get his bed moving across the room.

For the third time that weekend, Gavin had a plan.

He began to rock himself backwards and forwards. If only he could reach the chest of drawers he might pull his torch on to the bed. It lay there, half hidden by an old jersey.

He strained forwards. The ropes cut into his legs and wrists. He stretched his bound hands forward. They were just short of the top of the chest of drawers.

Gavin began to get desperate. Every minute counted.

"I've got to chance it that the Clan are on their way up Dumyat," he thought. "The house is only in view for part of the way. Once they are in the cave, they'll probably not open the shutter. They'll just sit there, waiting for me coming."

He began to rock the bed again, trying hard not to make too much noise. To his joy, the wooden bed shifted a little, giving a loud creak.

Gavin looked apprehensively at the door. He sat silently for a few minutes, but no one came.

He rocked the bed again. This time it moved a little more. About three or four inches, thought Gavin. But enough to reach the chest of drawers.

Again, he strained forward. His finger tips brushed the jersey, then swept it aside. His hands grasped the torch, awkwardly but surely. He brought it down carefully into his chest, then relaxed slightly on the bed.

He switched the beam on, being careful not to let it shine out of the window. A ray of light struck the far wall, lighting the room for an instant. It was a powerful torch.

"Now for it," thought Gavin. He looked at the dark blue oblong of the night sky, with the black mass of the hills filling half the shape.

His eyes focused on the sharp shape of Dumyat. He tried to judge where the path would be.

He pointed the torch towards the hill and began to press the switch. Three short flashes, then a gap. Then three long flashes, then a gap. Then another three short ones.

Gavin counted to ten before he pressed the switch again. The room lit up for a moment as he sent another three signals towards the hill. Short, short, short. Long, long, long. Short, short, short. The SOS signal. The distress signal used by sailors.

Surely the Clan would see the flashes and hurry back to the house to see what was happening. Clare would have the sense not to go blundering in, thought Gavin. She would approach with caution.

Gavin's wrists began to ache. Just then a loud booming noise came from the floor below. Gavin gasped. They had blown the safe.

He listened intently. After a bit he could hear raised voices. He sat very still, expecting any minute to hear the noise of the gang's car being driven away.

Nothing happened. No doors banged. Nothing more was said.

Gavin breathed again. The first attempt to open the safe must have failed. How long did that give him? He thought hard. Probably another hour. No more. Very probably, only half an hour.

Desperately he turned to the window again and with aching wrists continued to send his signal to the silent hills.

Gavin sat silently on the bed. The torch lay on the floor.

He was near to tears. His wrists and fingers were sore. So were his legs where the rope had cut in as he had tried to move.

Gavin felt in despair. The torch had been his last hope. It seemed to him that he had flashed for hours. Then the torch had flickered a little and had gone out.

The battery must have run out, he thought. He had used it quite a lot in the cave with the Clan. Now all was lost.

Any moment now he expected to hear a second explosion as the gang finally opened the safe.

His head ached.

He sat silently, lost in his thoughts.

At that moment there came a tap on the window.

20 The Clan Returns

Three silent figures wended their way up the hillside. Clare led the way, picking her way up the path which led to the upper slopes of Dumyat and the Clan cave. They moved quickly, with the easy sure-footed gait of the born hill-dweller.

Then Michael broke the silence. "Stop a minute, Clare," he said. "I'm puffed."

"So am I," said Mot.

"Fine pair of softies, you are," said Clare. "You've come up here dozens of times without a stop."

"I know, Clare," said Michael. "But we're tired. We've hardly been in bed in two nights."

"That's true," said Clare. "I don't suppose it matters now anyway. We've lost the contest."

She glanced at her watch. The luminous hands showed a quarter to twelve.

"I expect Gavin's at the cave already," she said. "By the time we get up there it will be midnight — and the contest will be over."

"He was cleverer than we thought," said Michael.

"He's good fun," said Mot. "I don't mind him being in the Clan. He put up a good show. I was certain we would catch him."

Clare sighed. "Yes," she said grudgingly. "His false hut was a good idea. That clinched it. It gave him enough time to evade us."

Mot nodded in the darkness. "We were too soft," he said. "We should have grabbed him then."

"Och, he might have dodged us in the trees," said Clare. "It's no use crying over spilt milk. Come on, we'd better get going. We've a long way to go yet."

The three began to move slowly up the path again.

"Clare!" exclaimed Mot, suddenly.

"What?"

"Look at that light flashing. Down there."

Mot pointed over the dark woods towards Gavin's house. The others followed his pointing finger.

Sure enough, a light flashed. Three short flashes. Then a pause. Then three long flashes, then another gap. Then another three short flashes. They could see it quite distinctly, winking away in the darkness.

"That's odd," said Clare. "It's so late there isn't another light showing anywhere."

"Perhaps it's just a motor cycle going along the road," said Michael.

"Don't be an idiot," said Clare. "It's a light from one spot. It's like a signal of some kind."

"It might be Gavin," said Michael.

"You might be right," said Clare.

"Do you think it's another trick to draw us away from the cave?" said Mot.

The Clan pondered this for a moment.

"I don't think it can be," said Michael. "After all, the contest is nearly over. If he was on his way to the cave it would hardly be sporting to grab him now. He's managed to stay free for nearly all the contest. All except for actually walking up to the cave," he added.

While they talked they continued to watch the light. It winked away, sending its short and long flashes.

"I think it must be Gavin," said Clare. "Perhaps his aunt made him stay in the house."

"It certainly looks as if it is from his house," said Mot. "I've been working it out. It's definitely from that area."

It was then that Michael covered himself in glory.

"It's Morse code," he said excitedly. "That's what it is! It's Morse code! Long and short signals. Look, see for yourselves."

Clare studied the flashes.

"Three short, three long, three short ... then a pause," she said. "It's the SOS signal! The distress

114

signal! Something's up! It must be Gavin. Perhaps it's the only Morse letters he knows."

"What shall we do, Clare!" asked Mot.

"Do?" said Clare. "Why, let's go down and find out. If it isn't him, we'll just have to come back up to the cave."

"I think we should go carefully," said Michael. "We don't know what it is. I'm sure Gavin wouldn't send an SOS signal just for a joke. He struck me as being a sensible fellow."

"You're right, Michael," said Mot. "I think we should go very slowly when we are near the house."

"Yes, that's the best plan," said Clare. "But, remember, I give the orders!"

"We'll trot down to the woods, and slow down near the house," she continued. "Then we stalk forward. But we'll have another conference near the house. Okay, let's get going."

With one accord, the three paused for a moment and examined the signal

Just then it went out ... and stayed out. The darkness appeared to close in on them all. The woods appeared slightly more sinister and menacing than before.

"Here we go," said Clare. "Stay close together."

Like the hillmen of old, the three Clansmen set off at a steady mile-eating trot-run down the path.

The Clan lay panting on the ground, lying like black shadows in the roots of a huge pine tree.

The woods were black, shot with silver light from the moon which popped in and out of drifting cloud.

Clare got her breath first.

"Two more minutes," she gasped. "Then we'll find out what has been happening. We'll make too much racket like this. Whew, what a trip!"

Halfway down the hill, the Clan had decided they had better speed things up. Their trot down the path had reached a full gallop by the time they reached the wood, and slowed to a quiet jog-trot along familiar paths.

When they had neared the strip of woodland which separated them from Gavin's house, Clare had waved them down. Mot and Michael had sank panting on the ground.

They looked like black spaniels, thought Clare, eyeing the heaving bodies. Eventually, their breath grew normal.

"Action stations!" said Clare. "There's something up, so let's go quietly and spy out the land. Stay together for the moment."

She began to pick her way slowly through the trees, gliding like a black shadow. Michael and Mot followed her in single file, carefully staying close behind her.

Occasionally, Clare would halt, hold a swaying branch in her hand and pass it to the next Clan member before going on. Michael, coming up in the rear, would then let it gently slide back to its original position.

They were doing that very difficult thing: silent movement through woodland at night.

Clare waved her hand. Immediately, all three sank down.

They were on the very edge of the trees.

21 The Owl's Call

Clare peered through the bushes, then inched slowly, very slowly, forwards until her head almost cleared the long grass at the edge of the woods. In front of her, the lawn of Gavin's house ran smoothly back towards the building.

Again, Mot and Michael crept up beside her. No word was exchanged. Three pairs of eyes swept over the ground ahead.

The moon came out from behind the clouds and lit up the house. Nothing was to be seen. Just the black of the building. No lights. No noise.

"That's funny," said Clare. "It *seems* very quiet."

She turned to Michael. "Try an owl call," she said. "Gavin's keen on birds. He'll hear that all right from the house. He might stick his head out a window."

Michael put his hand to his mouth. The sharp "kee-wick, kee-wick" of the tawny owl rang out.

The house was as silent as before.

Then Mot spoke: "Clare, there's something at the end of the house. Look, that black thing at the edge."

Clare peered forward. "So there is," she said.

She pondered for a moment. "Go and have a look, Mot," she said. "But be careful. Don't let yourself be seen."

Mot vanished into the darkness. A few minutes later he was back. He was in a state of high excitement.

"It's a car," he said. "And more than that, there's a man at an upstairs window looking out. He didn't see me. I tried the house door ... and it's locked."

"A man?" said Clare, witheringly. "That'll be Gavin's uncle."

"No, it wasn't," said Mot hotly. "I know what his uncle looks like. The moon shone on the window, and I could see he wore a cap. He seemed to have something over his face as well. Gavin's uncle never wears a cap. It looked a bit like a mask, but I couldn't see very well."

Clare thought again. "Let's all take a look," she said. "You lead on, Mot. You know the way."

Mot began to crawl the way he had gone before, this time with more confidence. He knew that there were no overhanging branches or dried twigs which would crackle and break.

Keeping close to the trees, but hidden by the foot-high long grass at the edge of the lawn the three Clansmen made their way round to the front of the house.

"Easy now," whispered Clare. "Hold it there, Mot," she said. "I'll take over now."

Mot surrendered his lead without a word. The boys were used to Clare being the leader.

She continued to crawl until she found a clear space behind a bush. She studied the house. Michael and Mot gradually eased themselves upwards inch by inch until they too could peer through the bushes. Again, the six eyes swept the building.

At the top window, they could clearly see the head and shoulders of a man peering out. He was half-hidden by the curtain inside the room, but visible each time the moonlight lit up the house. He seemed to have some kind of cap on his head, and a kind of covering across his face.

"What's he up to?" said Clare. "What's going on? Do you think we should just barge up to the front door and hammer on it?"

The boys hissed their disapproval.

"Okay! Okay! Just a thought," said Clare.

"Why don't we go round to Gavin's room?" said Michael. "Mot could go up the ivy."

Mot nodded his agreement.

"There's a bright idea," said Clare. "If Gavin isn't there, we could even get in the window. There's something fishy going on."

"Yes, there must be," said Mot. "Gavin wouldn't have signalled SOS as a joke."

"We don't know it was Gavin," said Michael.

"Of course it was," said Mot. "Who else could it have been?"

"Quiet, you two," hissed Clare. "I've got an idea."

The boys fell silent. Clare's ideas were generally good.

"It's like this," she said. "There may be something wrong. If there is, we've got to find out what it is. If there's nothing wrong, we'll look a prize lot of fools barging around someone else's house in the dark. Particularly when we've lost the contest with Gavin anyway."

"I don't know who the man is," she went on. "But we'll soon know if he's up to no good."

She waved her hand a little, pointing out another gap in the bushes.

"Michael, slide along there. Keep absolutely still, and keep low. Mot and I will move along a bit so there's plenty of room between us. Then let go another owl call. His window is open a bit at the bottom. He'll hear that. If he dodges out of sight, we'll know he's up to no good."

Michael grinned. He was very proud of his owl call. The Clan separated, wriggling into their new positions. They were very careful.

Clare looked along the bushes. She could dimly make out Michael lying on the ground. Settling herself comfortably, she made sure she had a good view of the house.

"Signal him now, Mot," she said, never taking her eyes off the house.

Mot waved his hand slowly. Further along, Michael caught the white glimmer and crouched low. A sharp "kee-wick, kee-wick" rang out through the trees.

Clare watched intently. The figure at the window vanished. Clare grunted with satisfaction. The Clan kept their places, still maintaining their animal-like stillness.

The figure returned to the window, carefully peering out. To the Clan's delight, and Michael's suppressed mirth, a silent shape floated from a tree, banked in front of the house and flew into the woods.

"It's a real owl!" gurgled Michael.

"Quiet!" said Clare. "I hope he saw it. Good show, too. It'll quieten him down. He got the fright of his life when the first call came."

"Well, that's it," she said. "There's something up! Let's get round the back and up the ivy. Come on!"

As they left, she looked disdainfully towards the house.

"Idiot!" she said. "Jerking around like that. No wonder Mot saw him!"

She disappeared noiselessly into the darkness.

120

22 Up the Ivy

The Clan were back on the edge of the wood at the back of the house.

Their caution never deserted them. Before taking further action, they again examined every inch of the house for possible movement.

"It's all right," said Clare. "There's no one at this side. Take a look at the back door, Mot, before you try the ivy. We'll cover you from here."

"All right," said Mot.

He watched the clouds until the moon disappeared from sight and the darkness deepened. Then, crouching low, he quickly crossed the lawn.

By the time the moon popped out again, flooding the lawn with silver light, he was crouching in the shadows of the house wall. A few minutes later, when all was dark again, he came creeping back.

"No good!" he whispered. "The door is shut tight. So are all the downstairs windows. I can't see into the kitchen. The window's got thick glass on it. All the other rooms are empty. I tried to get a squint at Gavin's room, but all was quiet."

Clare thought for a moment. Then she gave crisp orders.

"Mot, you get up the ivy to Gavin's window. See what you can. Try and get in, if you can. We'll stay here. If you find anything definite, come back here and report."

"Right-ho," said Mot. "Suppose something happens? Do we have a scatter signal!"

"Yes," said Clare. "We'll give one owl's call for danger, and two calls for scatter. If we have to split up, we'll meet one hour from now at the large pine near Gavin's false hut."

The boys nodded. They knew the spot.

"If you hear the danger call when you're up the ivy," said Clare, "stay put. The chances are that anyone wandering around will miss you if you're up above them."

"Seems all right to me," said Mot.

"Best of luck, Mot," said Michael, as Mot — casting a practised eye at the moon disappearing once more behind the clouds — set off across the lawn.

Clare and Michael settled down to wait. They saw Mot reach the wall and begin the slow climb up the ivy. Then they lost him in the shadows.

Minutes passed. Clare shivered a little. The perspiration of the run down the hill and from crawling through the bushes was beginning to dry on her in the cool summer-night air.

Michael tapped her on the arm. "Here he comes," he said.

Sure enough, Mot was weaving his way across the lawn. He tumbled in among them and sank down on the ground.

"Quiet, you clot!" said Clare.

Mot was wildly excited.

"There's something going on all right!" he said, the words tumbling out of his mouth. "Gavin's in his room! I saw him! I waved to him through the glass!"

He drew breath, adding to the dramatic effect. "We've got to do something! Get the police or something!"

"Get the police?" said Clare. "Whatever for?"

"He's tied to his bed! Tied to the bed!" said Mot.

"You're joking. It's a joke," said Michael. "He's having us on."

"I'm not, I tell you!" insisted Mot. "I was up there. I tell you, I nearly fell off the ivy!"

"At first, I couldn't see anything," he went on. "You know what it's like. I couldn't make anything out at

first. Then the moon came out again. It shone into the room.''

He paused for breath again.

''Go on, go on!'' said Michael impatiently.

''Well, I got a good grip on the ivy and looked into the room. And there he was, sitting on the bed.''

''Sitting on the bed?'' said Clare. ''Sitting on the bed doing what?''

''Doing nothing,'' said Mot. ''That's just the point. I wondered why he didn't come to the window. He could see me there. Then I saw he was tied up.''

''His hands were tied, and his legs were tied to the bed,'' continued Mot. ''He tried to signal to me by nodding his head and indicating that he was tied. He tried to tell me something as well, but I couldn't hear him through the glass.''

''There's more,'' he added.

''Quick, you clot!'' said Clare. ''We've no time to lose. What else did you see?''

''The window catch had been forced over,'' said Mot. ''I could see it. Do you remember the night I put the fiery cross in his room? The window opened easily then. It was one of these flick-back catches. Now this one has been jammed. The window wouldn't open. When I tried, I could see Gavin shaking his head.''

Clare thought briefly.

''We've got to get into that room,'' she said. ''And quick! But we've got to be quiet. And we've got to get help.''

''Michael,'' Clare said, ''get back to our house. Wake up Dad, and get him to phone the police. We may be making idiots of ourselves, but we've got to take a chance. If we can get into the room — and it's only all a joke — then we can phone the house and stop you. If we don't phone, get the police! Tell them everything we've seen.''

''You're right,'' said Michael. ''The whole set-up seems fishy to me.''

"Tell them everything," said Clare. "The car, the man at the window, the signal, Gavin being tied up. Pile it on! If there's something wrong, they've got to get here quickly. Off you go, Michael."

"Don't worry, I'll tell them," said Michael. "Dad will look very surprised though when I bang on his bedroom door."

"Och, don't bother about him," said Clare. "This is serious. Get cracking, Michael! We may not have much time. We don't know if whoever is in the house will leave or not."

"Right," said Michael. "I'm off!" He vanished into the darkness.

"Come on, Mot," said Clare. "Let's go over to the wall again."

"I'm beginning to get familiar with this lawn," said Mot. "It's the third time I've crossed it tonight."

"Quiet!" said Clare. This is no time for wisecracks."

They hurried across the lawn until they were huddled in the shadows below Gavin's window. Mot fished in his pocket.

"What are you doing?" said Clare.

"Making sure I've got my knife," said Mot. "I'll try it on the window catch, and see if I can force it open without too much noise." He held up a small sheath-knife.

"That won't be much use," said Clare. "The blade will snap. Try my gully."

She drew out a tough-looking clasp-knife, with a blade along one side and a thick spike on the other.

"It'll be all right," said Mot. "I'll have a go with this first. It's pretty tough."

He clambered up the ivy, stepping lightly from branch and tendril where it clung to the wall. The ivy shook and rustled, but remained in position.

Clare peered upwards. Then she heard a snapping sound. A whispered "dash it" came from above, and a piece of metal fell on the ground at her feet. It was the blade of Mot's knife.

Clare sighed. Mot came clambering down the ivy.

"Sorry, Clare," he said. "I thought I could do it. Whoever jammed the window simply bent the catch right over. It won't move, but it's pretty old and might snap off."

Clare held out her gully knife, spike first, without saying a word.

Again Mot set off up the ivy. The leaves swayed and rustled. Then, suddenly, came a loud crack.

Clare froze, gazing warily around. Nothing happened. Then a voice floated down.

"It broke off, Clare," said Mot. "Wait there. I'm going in."

23 The Open Safe

Gavin nearly wept when he saw Mot coming through the window. He had been sitting speechless watching Mot working at the catch. His heart had sunk when Mot's knife had broken.

He had started to get really worried when the catch broke. He sat very still, craning his ears in case Cobra and the other man heard the noise and came to investigate.

Then the window was lifted up quietly, and Mot's grinning face looked over the sill.

"Hello, there!" he said quietly.

"Mot!" said Gavin, thankfully.

"Quick! Untie me! We've got to raise the alarm. There are men in the house! They're after Uncle's silver."

The sentences tumbled out, one after the other.

"Uncle Fergus and Betty are tied up! They're trying to blow open the safe. They've already had one go! Quick! We've got to get the police."

"It's all right," said Mot. "Michael's gone back to the farm to waken Dad and to phone. I'll soon get you untied."

He sawed away at the ropes with Clare's gully knife, until Gavin could wriggle his hands and legs free.

"Where's Clare?" said Gavin, hurriedly getting to his feet and rubbing his chafed wrists and ankles.

"She's down below," said Mot. "I'll fetch her up."

"Hurry! Hurry!" said Gavin in a fever of excitement. "They may blow the safe at any minute. We've got to work out a way to stop them."

"Clare will think of something," said Mot.

He hurried to the window and leaned out. He turned back to Gavin.

"She's coming up. The ivy's a bit shaky for her. Just a sec."

He unfastened his anorak. Gavin could see he had a light rope coiled round his waist.

"Always carry this on big jobs," said Mot nonchalantly.

Quickly he tied one end to the bed and lowered it to the ground. A few minutes later, Clare's head appeared at the window.

"Hello, Gavin," she said calmly, although she was anything but calm.

"Hello, Clare," he said.

He almost felt like crying with relief. With the Clan there he felt they had a chance.

Clare wasted no time. "Is your door locked?" she asked Gavin.

"Yes," said Gavin. "They locked it and took the key."

"How many men are in the house? What are they up to?" snapped Clare.

"Four," said Gavin. "They're after the silver. Can't we stop talking and do something?"

"I know, I know!" said Clare. "I just want a picture of what's going on. Quickly, now!"

"They must have broken in here," said Gavin. "They tied Uncle Fergus and Betty up. They grabbed me when I went into the house for a moment. They tried to blow the safe open but it didn't work. They're going to try again any minute now. If they get in, they'll be off with the silver."

Clare thought quickly. She looked at the faces of the two boys as they huddled together. All three were whispering.

"Michael's gone for the police," she said. "If Dad gets hold of Constable Mackenzie at his house they'll come through the woods. He's our local policeman, Gavin. That's quicker than going round by road."

"To be on the safe side," went on Clare, "someone